The Other Woman

EXPLORING THE STORY OF HAGAR

By JoAnn Streeter Shade

OTHERS PRESS

The Salvation Army
USA Eastern Territory
West Nyack, New York
2011

The Other Woman, Exploring the Story of Hagar by JoAnne Streeter Shade.

Art Direction: Keri Johnson
Design: Karena Lin

Others Press
The Salvation Army
440 West Nyack Rd.
West Nyack, NY 10994

FIRST EDITION

Poems signed "jas" are by JoAnn Shade.

ISBN: 978-0-89216-128-7

Printed in the United States of America.

Endorsements

Major JoAnn Shade's engaging, down–to–earth style and years of personal experience breathe life into the story of Hagar, the slave–girl of Sarah. Written with wit and warmth, intelligence and deep faith, this book will be a delight for anyone who has ever thought about the meaning of Hagar's experiences, or questioned an injustice, or struggled with God's treatment of the oppressed and downtrodden, or wondered why God has not answered their prayers the way they had hoped. It is written for those who, like Major Shade, are seeking to understand and live their own lives in light of scripture and will be especially meaningful for women, and those who have experienced injustice, fear, and abuse. It would be excellent as a women's, adults' or young adults' Bible study, or Sunday school or book club or retreat text. Major Shade's candid questions and examples bring readers into a conversation with the story and with their own faith–lives that is at once comforting and challenging, reassuring and stimulating.

The Other Woman: Exploring the Story of Hagar is written from the perspective of a woman who has served her Lord faithfully through trials and joys and who has witnessed firsthand the themes found in Hagar's story. Using illustrations from her preaching, teaching, and counseling ministry and her own life, Major Shade becomes the reader's companion on a phrase–by–phrase exploration of the text. Divided into 38 brief, easily assimilated chapters and enhanced by poetry, quotations and scriptural examples, this book is lovely, accessible, and sometimes surprising. Major Shade's common–sense approach to scriptural interpretation and her confident, well–informed guidance leads her readers to eye–opening twists and connections. Perseverance, escape, obedience, oppression, fear, courage, birthing, grief, and hope are just a few of the themes emerging from Major Shade's careful and creative study.

This book is like an extended and beloved sermon, preached by a favorite pastor—one that will be read again and again to remind us of God's nature and will and the challenge of living in faith through difficult times. After reading this book, Major Shade's readers will give Hagar and her story a new, prominent, and valued place in their faith–lives.

—Rev. Dr. Sue Dickson
Ashland University

How often have you felt like Hagar, rejected, forgotten or betrayed? How often have life's disappointments left you searching for God's empathy, justice, and redemption? JoAnn Shade enters Hagar's painful journey to show that it is precisely in places of despair that we find God's warmest embrace and new paths of redemption.

—Mimi Haddad
President, Christians for Biblical Equality

In this well–written book, Major Shade takes the reader on a memorable and meaningful journey, drawing helpful lessons from Hagar's story—sometimes mining gold out of a short phrase or a single word. She touches on a vast range of subjects, from abuse and pregnancy and revenge to single parenting, abandonment, grief, and more ... There is much to take away from this book—and not for women only. Any seeking soul, any student of the Bible, anyone who is craving hope and encouragement, will profit from it.

—Bob Hostetler
Award–winning author of 26 books

Through Hagar's story, JoAnn Streeter Shade enables us to hear the voice of the downtrodden, witness the struggles of the despairing, and encounter with fresh eyes the compassion of the God Who Sees. In this wonderful, warm, and sometimes whimsical reading, Hagar emerges from Abraham's shadow to speak of the pain of exclusion and give hope and assurance to those who travel difficult paths. Shade writes with insight, wisdom, and a flair for the poetic that draws us in to Hagar's story in ways that illuminate both the biblical vision and our own lives and faith. I heartily recommend this book!

—L. Daniel Hawk
Ashland Theological Seminary

JoAnn Shade reaches with compassion and wisdom into the souls of women as she guides readers through a deep reading of the Hagar story. This is a wonderful resource for the Church.

—Elaine Heath, Ph.D.
Perkins School of Theology

JoAnn Streeter Shade has delved deeply into the book of Genesis, exploring the story of Hagar. The result, as one would expect from JoAnn, makes compelling reading. Hagar's life becomes relevant and challenging to all ages and cultures. Abram and Sarai also have a major part in the narrative. I very much enjoyed the book. It is a carefully and beautifully written study and I know others will be eager to read it.

—Commissioner Helen Clifton,
Retired World President of Women's Ministries, The Salvation Army

Major Shade provides a unique glimpse into the life of an often–neglected biblical character—Hagar. She weaves her own personal vision with keen exegetical insight to develop a portrait that is both ancient and new. Shade not only establishes an empathetic connection with this remarkable woman but also gives hope to all who need to know the 'God who sees.' Like Hagar, the reader is drawn into the healing presence of the divine.

—Dr. Paul Chilcote
Ashland Theological Seminary

Genesis 16

Now Sarai, Abram's wife, bore him no children. She had an Egyptian slave–girl whose name was Hagar, and Sarai said to Abram, "You see that the Lord has prevented me from bearing children; go in to my slave–girl; it may be that I shall obtain children by her." And Abram listened to the voice of Sarai. So, after Abram had lived ten years in the land of Canaan, Sarai, Abram's wife, took Hagar the Egyptian, her slave–girl, and gave her to her husband Abram as a wife. He went in to Hagar, and she conceived; and when she saw that she had conceived, she looked with contempt on her mistress. Then Sarai said to Abram, "May the wrong done to me be on you! I gave my slave–girl to your embrace, and when she saw that she had conceived, she looked on me with contempt. May the Lord judge between you and me!" But Abram said to Sarai, "Your slave–girl is in your power; do to her as you please." Then Sarai dealt harshly with her, and she ran away from her.

The angel of the Lord found her by a spring of water in the wilderness, the spring on the way to Shur. And he said, "Hagar, slave–girl of Sarai, where have you come from and where are you going?" She said, "I am running away from my mistress Sarai." The angel of the Lord said to her, "Return to your mistress, and submit to her." The angel of the Lord also said to her, "I will so greatly multiply your offspring that they cannot be counted for multitude." And the angel of the Lord said to her,

"Now you have conceived and shall bear a son; you shall call him Ishmael [God hears], for the Lord has given heed to your affliction. He shall be a wild ass of a man, with his hand against everyone, and everyone's hand against him, and he shall live at odds with all his kin." So she named the Lord who spoke to her, "You are El–roi," [the God who sees] for she said, "Have I really seen God and remained alive after seeing him?" Therefore the well was called Beer–lahai–roi [the Well of the Living One who sees me]; it lies between Kadesh and Bered.

Hagar bore Abram a son; and Abram named his son, whom Hagar bore, Ishmael. Abram was eighty–six years old when Hagar bore him Ishmael.

Genesis 21:8–21

The child [Isaac, born to Abraham and Sarah] grew, and was weaned; and Abraham made a great feast on the day that Isaac was weaned. But Sarah saw the son of Hagar the Egyptian, whom she had borne to Abraham, playing with her son Isaac. So she said to Abraham, "Cast out this slave woman with her son; for the son of this slave woman shall not inherit along with my son Isaac." The matter was very distressing to Abraham on account of his son. But God said to Abraham, "Do not be distressed because of the boy and because of your slave woman; whatever Sarah says to you, do as she tells you, for it is through Isaac that offspring shall be named for you. As for the son of the slave woman, I will make a nation of him also, because he is your offspring." So Abraham rose early in the morning, and took bread, and a skin of water, and gave it to Hagar, putting it on her shoulder, along with the child, and sent her away. And she departed, and wandered about in the wilderness of Beer-sheba.

When the water in the skin was gone, she cast the child under one of the bushes. Then she went and sat down opposite him a good way off, about the distance of a bowshot; for she said, "Do not let me look on the death of the child." And as she sat opposite him, she lifted up her voice and wept. And God heard the voice of the boy; and the angel of God called to Hagar from heaven, and said to her, "What troubles you, Hagar? Do not be afraid; for God has heard the voice of the boy where he is. Come, lift up the boy and hold him fast with your hand, for I will make a great nation of him." Then God opened her eyes, and she saw a well of water. She went, and filled the skin with water, and gave the boy a drink.

God was with the boy, and he grew up; he lived in the wilderness, and became an expert with the bow. He lived in the wilderness of Paran; and his mother got a wife for him from the land of Egypt.

Table of Contents

Getting Acquainted

Now Sarai, Abram's wife, bore him no children.
She had an Egyptian slave–girl whose name was Hagar ...

Hagar? Who is Hagar? Only a supporting actress in the grand drama of Genesis (or so I thought), she has not had a sterling reputation over the years. She wandered through the margins of the narrative of Abraham and Sarah, and from what I could remember, she tended to cause trouble. So why choose Hagar for the subject of a book about hearing and seeing God? After all, she is a slave, an outcast, the other of Ishmael. She's not on the top ten list of Bible heroines. What could we possibly learn from Hagar? Wasn't Sarah the star of the Genesis drama?

For starters, Hagar is a gutsy woman who dared run away from an abusive situation, a listening woman who was willing to obey God even when it made no sense, and a seeking woman who named God. As the loser in a one–sided battle seemingly marked by envy and greed, the Egyptian slave–woman Hagar encounters God not once, but twice. Can you name any other biblical women—outside of those who walked with Jesus—who had that experience?

Are you hearing any echoes? Here is a woman who knew what it was like to be female in a patriarchal (male–dominated) society, an alien in a fiercely nationalistic tribe, and a slave–girl to a powerful, sometimes harsh woman. Are you starting to connect the dots? Hagar is in us, in the corners of our desperation, in the impetuous desire to escape, in the need to protect what we are birthing, and in our willingness to open our eyes and see God.

When I first began to spend time with her story, she was persistent: *I have much to teach you.* She invaded my dreams and colored my waking hours. *Pay attention to me*, she would nudge. I'd find myself asking, *Hagar, what are you trying to tell me?* And time after time, I'd find her story answering me: *Open your eyes, see God, drink from the well.* As Phyllis Trible affirms, "Belonging to a narrative that rejects her, Hagar is a fleeting yet haunting figure in Scripture … In many and varied ways, Hagar shapes and challenges faith."[1]

I want to invite you to join me as we dig deep into Hagar's story, considering it from many angles. We will see through Hagar's eyes, touch through Hagar's fingers, and weep through Hagar's tears. Now you may have learned this story in Sunday school as the story of Abraham and Sarah, but we will re–cast the players, so that Hagar plays the lead. Abraham and Sarah have a treasured place in the history of God's people, and we can continue to learn much from their examples. But Hagar too has much to say, and I trust that she will show us where to go, and how to see God in the process.

My initial reaction to Hagar's narrative was to write for women. After all, Hagar was a woman, I'm a woman, and much of her story revolves around her roles as a woman—Sarah's handmaiden, Abraham's concubine, Ishmael's mother. Yet Hagar's story reaches beyond gender, just as it reaches beyond ethnicity, age, and race. If men and women alike can learn from Abraham's narrative, we can also learn from Hagar's narrative. To relegate Hagar's story to the "chick flick" genre does her a great disservice. So while there are a few sections of this book that speak explicitly to women, particularly regarding sexuality, birthing, and wailing, the overarching principles found in those passages extend past gender.

As a note of explanation, for the sake of simplicity, we'll use one name for Hagar's master and mistress. At the beginning of the narrative, they are Abram and Sarai, but God gives them new names, Abraham and Sarah, with which we are more familiar, and except for the direct Scripture references, we will use their new names in the course of this book. The passages that directly apply to Hagar are provided for you, but you may want to read the entire story for perspective. It begins in Genesis 11:27 and concludes with the death of Abraham in Genesis 25. Unless otherwise noted, the text used is the New Revised Standard Version.

As I've shared my passion for Hagar's story, someone asked me, "Isn't Hagar the mother of Islam, just as Sarah is considered the mother of Judaism? Although it is true that Mohammed, the "founder" of Islam,

---

[1] Phyllis Trible, *Texts of Terror: Literary Feminist Reading of Biblical Narratives*. Philadelphia: Fortress Press, 1984, p. 27.

traces his roots back to Abraham through the line of Ishmael, son of Hagar and Abraham, the Islamic faith itself did not emerge until nearly 2,400 years after Abraham, Hagar, and Ishmael lived. Neither Hagar nor Ishmael had any direct role in the development of the Islamic faith, and their influence on that would be no more or less than Abraham's. Hagar is not the mother of Islam, nor is she mentioned by name in the Koran. She is, however, a woman who encountered God and speaks to us through her story.

As a final disclaimer of sorts, I will take some liberty with Hagar's story, while being faithful to the biblical text. I found myself using a lot of words like *perhaps, maybe,* and *it could be,* as I both heard her voice and allowed her narrative to come alive in my imagination. I invite you to join me as her story unfolds, to imagine what it might have been like to experience her journey, and to embrace her as a sister.

Through No Choice of Her Own

... an Egyptian slave–girl ...

Hagar lived in a culture in which a woman of her economic status and ethnicity (as a part of Abraham's household) was definitely a victim. She did not choose slavery. She did not choose to be born an Egyptian; she did not choose to be without resources of her own; she did not choose to be dragged away from her homeland; and she did not choose to wait hand and foot upon a harsh woman, in a life that held no hope for the future. No, Hagar chose none of these circumstances, nor did she deserve to be in those circumstances. If Hagar were living in our 21st–century's culture of victimization, she would deserve to wear the crown jewels of victimhood. Life was not easy for this woman.

I have great sympathy for Hagar. I struggle to imagine what it would be like to live as a slave to another. There are those among my friends whose ancestors knew the lash of the overseer's whip and who watched in utter helplessness as their children were sold to a plantation down the river. It is in their blood, this heritage of slavery, of forced labor, and as the family stories are passed down, the heart knows. While this story is not my own, the stories speak. No, we do not have to turn to Hagar's time to know the price of slavery.

Yet we have our own chains of slavery in our day. Worldwide, women and children are still trafficked for cheap employment and sexual favors. I have sisters who live with men who are abusive to them. These women are enslaved. They know that if they leave, their men will stalk them, and it's just too much, too dangerous, to think of escape. Less terrorizing but just as enslaving are the excessive mortgage payments, the addictions to alcohol or power or crack, and the glittering images that we cling to for dear life. Yes, we have our own garments of slavery.

There are those who are free from these types of restraints but have few economic resources. Poverty brings its own handcuffs of enslavement.

When a person has no place to sleep and isn't sure where the next meal will come from, too much energy must be used to hustle a few bucks or to locate the soup kitchen that serves meals the second Friday of the month, only between 11:45 a.m. and 12:30 p.m. When the very basics of human living are uncertain, hope is in short supply, and there is no sense in delaying gratification because the view of the future is so hazy. Survival for today is the goal. I have worked among the poor for more than 30 years. I have witnessed terrible circumstances and tragic consequences firsthand. I know of man's inhumanity to man, woman's inhumanity to woman, and abuse that crosses gender (and economic) lines. Life is difficult.

On some level, all people are legitimately victims, for we have all suffered or experienced loss or injustice of some kind. The list is endless: ethnicity, poverty, illness, abuse, violence, abandonment, addiction, despair, death. Add to these the sorrow caused by natural disasters such as the tsunami of 2004, Hurricane Katrina, and the Haitian earthquake. The magnitude is overwhelming, the depth of grief unfathomable. Picture 10 women waiting in a hospital to prove that the one surviving infant is the baby who was ripped from her arms by the monster wave in Indonesia, and you can see agony.

We each bear wounds that need to be tended to, bandaged, and healed. Scars need time and space to form. And in the midst of the pain, God knows and God sees. That is why Malachi promised that the sun of righteousness would arise with healing in his wings. God hears the cries of his people. God heard the distress of Hagar.

But, as we will see, Hagar's distress is not the end of the story. There comes a time when she must open her eyes, dry her tears, get up from her place of sorrow, and move. Even in this early biblical narrative, we see the pattern: God hears, but the woman, the man must move. Jacob wrestles. Joseph flees. Jael picks up a stake. The widow of Zarephath bakes. The bleeding woman reaches for a hem. (For the rest of these stories, see Genesis 32 [Jacob], Genesis 39–40 [Joseph], Judges 4–5 [Jael], I Kings 17 [widow of Zarephath], and Mark 5 [bleeding woman]).

As destructive and devastating as this ache can be, we cannot build a life with God based solely on our pain. The roots have no strength. They rot in the excess of our tears, poisoned by the toxins given off as they fester. They use up all the nutrients of the soil to feed themselves. The roots can't get past the stony ground.

The danger is that pain cannot remain as pure pain. Remember your eighth–grade biology class? A living organism either grows or decays. It moves toward life or death, for it cannot stay the same. Pain sinks into bitterness, when our anger overwhelms us and colors all our relationships. It moves onto Envy Street, where we are jealous of someone who is seemingly living a charmed life. (Hagar, you must remember that life for Sarah has not been a walk in the park either!) We allow the strings of victimhood to bind us into a learned helplessness that becomes a straitjacket. And one way or another, everybody in the house pays.

I've had lots of conversations about pain and sorrow and the victims they capture, and I've read quite a bit on the subject as well. Two thoughts have emerged from the anguish, and have both expanded my understanding and given me insight into my own life story. Henri Nouwen, a Catholic priest who left an impressive teaching, writing and speaking career to care for a profoundly handicapped young man, wrote from his own experience:

> Understanding our wounds is not enough. Finally we must find the freedom to step over our wounds and the courage to forgive those who have wounded us. Have the courage to trust that you won't fall into an abyss of nothingness but into the safe embrace of a God whose love will heal all your wounds.[2]

A trusted friend uttered one sentence that has echoed in me for years: *You must find something or someone that matters more than your pain.* I know the truth of these words, and I know the lead in my bones, the whimper that cries, "I just can't do it." And then God comes, and he sees. He speaks, and we lift up our heads, in desperation, in curiosity, and in faith. We see God, we see a well of water, we see what we have birthed. We listen and we answer. We stand and we begin to move with all we can manage, that first baby step.

Hang in on this. By the end of our interaction with Hagar's story,

---

[2] Henri J. Nouwen, *Here and Now: Living in the Spirit.* New York: The Crossroads Publishing Company, 1996, p. 45.

she will have helped us to balance our need to face what is troubling us, as well as the harm we do to others, with the possibilities that are before us. For in spite of all her struggles and what's seen by some as a tarnished reputation, Hagar's is a story of hope. The Lord is *El–roi*, the God who sees. He saw Hagar, and, in seeing her, he sees us.

Given Away

Sarai gave her (Hagar) to her husband for his wife.

By the second line of Hagar's story, we are face–to–face with an image that's difficult to wrap our arms around. As a woman, an Egyptian, and a slave, Hagar had a difficult enough life, and now she was to be the wife (concubine) of an 85–year–old man. I wonder if Hagar heard Abraham and Sarah talking in the night about Abraham's encounter with the Lord God and the promise of descendants as numerous as the stars (Gen. 15:5). She certainly would have known that Sarah was past the time of child–bearing—she did the wash each month (Gen. 18:11). *Hagar, did you sense Sarah's gaze upon you as she contemplated her options, wondering whether your womb might be fertile? How she might use you to get what she wanted? Did Abraham look upon you with a lecherous grin, an inviting smile, or with a sense of resignation to what seemed like the only option left to him?*

From the account in Scripture, we have no idea of Hagar's reaction to this plan, for we only know that Abraham did as he was told. When she turned away from Abraham after he had planted his seed in her womb, did she see it as a step up, an honor to have slept with the master? Was she pragmatic in her thinking, recognizing that she now would gain status in the household? Or did she sense the offense against her body that a contemporary woman would experience?

For in truth, her body had been invaded to satisfy the needs of another (both Abraham and Sarah). Whatever she felt, a slave's feelings didn't matter. Her mistress had directed Hagar to Abraham's tent, and she went. In fact, by sharing his bed, she became Abraham's wife (a second wife, of course, perhaps known as a concubine, with greater status than a slave–girl but still considerably beneath Sarah, the first wife).

There are at least four components to this act that are foreign to our culture. First, arranged marriages just don't happen in 21st–century America. No, we "fall in love" and marry the person of our dreams, and half of us say good–bye to our dream when the marriage disintegrates. Perhaps the closest Americans come to arranged marriage is a dating service or website that promises compatibility. No, we choose whom we will marry.

Second, bigamy is against the law, and there is a serious wisdom in this law of our land. I cannot imagine sharing my husband with another woman, although having someone else to do the housework would have its benefits. A young client had the experience of living with her husband and his girlfriend. He had moved out and left town with another woman, but because the wife wanted him to have contact with the children (and didn't want to give him up), she followed him and moved in with him.

Every time we talked, there was a new story about the interactions between the wife and the woman we ended up calling the wife–in–law. It was confusing for the children, humiliating for their mother, awkward at best for the second woman, and required a tremendous balancing act from the man in the triangle. He didn't handle his situation well at all. Their story was a huge dose of reality that convinced me once again that the one man/one woman model is definitely God's idea for marriage.

And then we find surrogate parenting. While in recent years this has become a bit of a trend, it is still outside the norm in our culture. When it is done, it is either due to a great love (like the mother in her 50s who carried twins for her daughter) or a hefty payment. Apparently rather common in Old Testament times (and not the choice of the woman bearing the child), in today's world it is rare, and can be difficult, when the surrogate struggles to release the baby she has carried and nourished for nine months.

But the biggest difference in Western culture is that a woman is responsible for her sexual availability. If she does not want to have intercourse with a man, she is protected by both law and custom, and if he persists, he can be charged with rape. I've had interesting discussions about this with my teenage son around the Kobe Bryant case. We talked about when a "yes" becomes a "no" and the need for men to understand that. Also, with the advent of the pill and other methods of birth control, the woman is deemed responsible for her reproductive capacity. It is her body, after all, says our culture.

Yes, in an ideal world a woman does have the ability to control her sexual life. But we don't live in an ideal world. In the United States, one out of three women is sexually abused by the age of 18. In writing about the reasons women become and remain welfare recipients, Jason DeParle recognizes that "talk of childhood molestation has arisen with eerie regularity." One Oregon woman told DeParle, "I don't call it anything special, because it seems like it happens to everybody."[3] But those who are sexually abused as children are more likely to abuse alcohol or drugs, suffer from depression, or become victims of domestic violence as adults.

Many girls wrongly believe that the only way to get the man they want is to "put out" sexually. Abstinence movements preach that "true love waits," but we invite hundreds of voices into our living rooms that bombard our senses with the message, "Just do it." Sexual activity becomes a rite of passage for young teens, and being a virgin at 15 or 16 can bring a loss of status within the neighborhood circle. We don't understand that when we sleep with a guy, we are sleeping with the ghosts (and germs) of every girl he's ever slept with. And at 15 or 16, we don't know that every sexual encounter we have tears a deeper rip in our souls.

Abraham's tent does look inviting. A powerful man, with lots of resources, Abraham offered a way out—a way up—to Hagar. Perhaps the transition from servant–girl to wife seemed like the best thing to come along since sliced bread. If indeed she was being forced into his tent, she might as well make the best of it.

Do we rationalize in the same way, choosing between the lesser of two evils or the temptation of the present moment rather than looking past the open flap of the tent to the self–respect we can have by saying "no"? A lonely 35–year–old woman chooses a man who she knows isn't healthy for her, but she can't face the risk of being alone forever. An overweight teenage girl, overwhelmed by the attention of her next–door neighbor, ignores his groping hands and prison record in order to have someone tell her she's pretty.

The difference between Hagar and us is that we do have a choice. The beckoning fingers of our culture, while enticing, do not bear the absolute life and death power that Sarah had over Hagar. We can stay

[3] Jason DeParle, *American Dream: Three Women, Ten Kids, and a Nation's Drive to End Welfare.* New York: Viking Penguin, 2004, p. 218.

out of the tent of casual sexual activity. We can wait until the man who claims to love us proves that pledge through his actions, and ultimately, at the altar.

The beckoning finger of sexual desire does have the ultimate power of life and death, and we don't get it. We honor Hagar, we honor ourselves, and we honor God when we respect ourselves enough to refuse to enter Abraham's tent.

I Am with Child

He went in to Hagar, and she conceived ...

I remember the day our suspicion that we were going to have our third child was confirmed. Home pregnancy test kits had recently been introduced, and our 6–year–old reported the good news for show–and–tell: "The stick turned blue, so my mom's going to have a baby!" We were thrilled. But not every pregnancy is greeted with joy. Some women face a positive pregnancy test with ambivalence, while others respond with pure terror.

We can guess that Hagar's pregnancy brought her ambivalent feelings. *Ambivalent.* It means having conflicting feelings at the same time. Somehow the word is too weak for me. It conjures up images of wishy–washy feelings that seem willing to co–exist for a while, just floating around without causing too much trouble. I don't know where I got that impression—perhaps because its dictionary neighbor is *ambiguous* (not clear, vague). However, the thoughts and emotions that jostle around inside a newly pregnant woman are anything but wishy–washy.

I don't have what I need to have this baby. My husband is __________ (fill in the blank). *What husband? There isn't enough money. It's just not the right time. Do I have what it takes to be a mother? What will the birth of this child do to me? To my body? How can I ever love another? What if I can't love this baby? What if I don't know what to do with it? I'm just not ready. Will I lose a part of my self? I'm frightened.* The words escape from us unbidden or get buried under layers of denial. What do we do with them?

We speak them. In the solitude of the early morning, in the company of a trusted friend, in the groanings of our prayers, we allow them to form on our lips. We refuse to pretend that we have all the answers, but we allow the questions to arise and take shape. They can be faced in the light of day, but when confined to darkness, they take on a power too large for us to handle.

And we discover that we are not alone. Other women experience similar feelings and doubts. Even when a pregnancy is planned and welcome, we are never fully prepared for new life to grow within us. There is always an uncertainty, always a sense of mystery.

It brings me to the question that troubles me. For you see, I want to be charge of whatever I am birthing at any given time. I don't want the uncertainty. I want to be in charge of my children—keeping them safe, meeting their needs, and directing their paths. I want to control the other birthings in me—the ideas, the words, the music, the budding friendships, the new beginnings. No way do I want to "cast my bread upon the water" and release the outcome.

When delivering our third son, I hit a point after I had been pushing for some time when I couldn't take it any longer. I said to the midwife, "Let's forget about this for today. I'll go home and rethink this whole process."

But the trouble was that there was no turning back. The child must be born, released, let go. My body could no longer contain him. One day, Hagar must know, her child will be Abraham's—and Sarah's. One day, another woman will be claiming my son as her own. One day, someone else will be reading these words I am birthing. They will no longer belong to me. Hagar, Hannah (I Samuel), Elizabeth (Luke 1), and Mary (Luke 1–2)—they all knew the pain and joy of birth, and the anguish of letting go.

The Lord said to Eve in the Garden of Eden, "in pain you shall bring forth children" (Gen. 3:16). When we can fully comprehend the truth in this, we can begin to accept its implications to our lives. As we birth and raise children, we will experience pain. As we birth and raise our various hopes and dreams, we will also experience pain. It is what it is. But we can choose (that pesky word again) to anticipate what is coming, to breathe through the painful contractions, and to willingly release what is yearning to be birthed within us.

Getting Uppity

And when she saw that she had conceived, she looked with contempt on her mistress.

In the patriarchal economy of Hagar's world, fertility was the currency of choice, and now she had the goods. Because she was pregnant, her value just increased tenfold in the Abraham household. Yet she must have questioned what being a mother would look like in this triangle in which she had the least power of the three players.

I've been known to roll my eyes and cast a look of disdain at someone when I'm disgusted (my kids would describe it as the evil eye), and I am willing to plead guilty when I do that, but it disturbs me when I am accused of being contemptuous when I really haven't been. Hagar's treatment of Sarah is a situation in which we don't know for sure whether she was guilty of looking at Sarah with contempt, or whether this was an instance of Sarah's jealousy or her perception of something that wasn't there.

It does look as though Hagar further victimized herself in this encounter. She could have quietly gone about her business and carried the baby to term in the safety of Abraham's protection as his wife (Sarah's designation of her status). She could have cherished the child growing within her while quietly being grateful for her shifting status in the household. But the text indicates that there was a problem. Hagar "looked with contempt on her mistress" (Gen. 16:4). We have to wonder what happened between the two women. Did Hagar simply give in to her increased value and gloat over her pregnancy? Was this payback time for the way Sarah had treated her?

If it was, I understand. After all those years of being only the servant girl, finally Hagar was something more. Sarah, for all her power, wealth and status, is barren and Hagar is not. She is to be the mother of Abraham's child. The balance has shifted. Sarah is penniless, and now Hagar holds the full purse.

I've seen a shifting of economic status, such as when someone raised in poverty gets her first tax refund with her Earned Income Credit, perhaps as much as $5,000, or when the child support finally kicks in. When we've lived without for so long, we don't know what to do when we hold that check in our hands. Perhaps that is Hagar's dilemma. She's got the full purse, but she doesn't know what to do, so she goes with her instinct. *I've got the power now, so I'm going to get back at Sarah.*

The same is often true for us. Contempt is so strong and so destructive, yet we go there, and we feel so entitled to go there. We fall into the trap of thinking that in order for us to feel better about ourselves, we have to find a way to decrease the other person's value. Yet it doesn't help. We may feel better in the moment, but soon a spirit of bitterness begins to grow. In the meantime, the one whom we have "dissed" (disrespected, disregarded, demeaned, dismissed) knows it, and is likely to retaliate.

Perhaps Hagar also determined to manipulate the current situation to her benefit. *I'm going to do what will feel good for the moment because who knows what the future will bring—this may be my one chance to feel good about myself.* Think of the researcher who, rather than waiting for a second round of testing, simply manipulates the data just enough to obtain the desired results. It happens as well when the business associate twists the truth just enough to gain the promotion over her co–worker. We tend to grab at any hope of changing the outcome when we can see a sliver of possibility.

It could be as well that Hagar was just waiting for the chance to let her true nature come out. She may have been a vicious woman by nature who had had to hold that uppity attitude in check because she had no power. Hagar may have simply behaved poorly in this situation, and we cannot excuse the actions that come from a wicked heart.

What can we do when faced with the question of shifting power and value? Can we hope to find a measure of equality within a hierarchical structure? Can we take pride in our ideas, in the work we birth? When is it time to speak, to validate our experiences and feelings, and when is it time to be still? What of our own sin, when we feel contempt toward another and believe that contempt to be justified, or when we have a burning desire for revenge? What do we do when faced with a supervisor (or elder) who is simply unjust?

And why does it seem to be more difficult to work for another woman, when we would truly like to work as a team? Biblical scholar

Phyllis Trible, in writing about Sarah and Hagar, senses our yearning: "This unexpected twist provides an occasion for mutuality and equality between two females, but it is not to be."[4] They could have put their differences aside, sat down and figured it out, but they didn't.

In Hagar's case, she may have misjudged the value of her pregnancy and her power to manipulate the circumstances to her benefit, because in the end, she did not prevail. Sarah went to Abraham, in good first–wife fashion, with her complaint: "May the wrong done to me be on you! I gave my slave–girl to your embrace, and when she saw that she had conceived, she looked on me with contempt. May the Lord judge between you and me" (Gen. 16:5).

And wouldn't you know, Abraham backed Sarah, the barren one. "Your slave–girl is in your power; do to her as you please" (Gen 16:6). Here Hagar becomes the pawn to be passed back and forth between Abraham and Sarah. In fact, Abraham seems to remove himself from this battle between the two women, telling Sarah that since this is her servant (notice he doesn't define Hagar as his wife in this exchange), she can handle it herself. And handle it she does.

What might have allowed Sarah and Hagar to stop the escalation of this incident? Had Paul's words to the Romans been available, they might have helped. "If it is possible, so far as it depends on you, live peaceably with all" (Romans 12:18). While these words appeared a few centuries too late for Hagar and Sarah, their direction is profound. When two people are in conflict, it is up to you, to me, to do what is within our ability to bring peace. That means if we must apologize, we apologize. If we have to give up our demand to be understood, we have to do that. No matter what the other does, whether Sarah, Abraham or Hagar, we are never off the hook as far as our behavior is concerned.

But there is another slant we can take on this story.

---

[4] Trible, p. 12.

Misunderstood

Her mistress was slight in her eyes ...

Is it possible that Hagar continued to be the innocent, the victim, in this drama? Renita Weems ponders this, wondering "whether Hagar's contempt for Sarah was real or imagined on Sarah's part, we can only guess."[5] Perhaps it was simply Hagar's expanding waistline that inspired Sarah's rage. The words used in the passage raise a doubt about Hagar's intent, and we know from experience that jealousy and envy can be deadly emotions when allowed to run rampant through the life of a woman—especially a woman in a precarious position of power—about to lose perceived status to a slave. The verb *(qll)* that is used has a number of meanings. It can be translated, "despise" or "look upon with contempt," but it can also mean "her mistress was slight in her eyes" or "was lowered in her esteem."[6]

Perhaps Hagar's intent was not contempt at all but merely a shifting of perspective as she began to see herself as a woman with value rather than as a worthless slave. Such is the mystery of the simple biblical phrase: that the modern reader can still only guess what was Hagar's behavior and her intent in this situation.

Oh, to be misunderstood and to have no recourse. Been there, done that. Being misunderstood can so easily lead us into deep waters. Consider the rip–roaring marital arguments resulting from phrases like these: *Don't look at me that way. I don't like the tone of your voice. Don't raise your voice to me. I saw the way you looked at the guy at the pharmacy last night.* Off we go, trying to prove to our spouse that he's got it wrong.

Or at work, the boss asks for our opinion and we offer it, hesitantly at first, but then with conviction, only to hear through the copy machine grapevine the next day that our enthusiasm was twisted to appear as if we were after someone else's job. We feel betrayed by our boss, by the gossip that will stick to us like glue, and by ourselves. We believed in

---

Renita J. Weems, *Just a Sister Away: A Womanist Vision of Women's Relationships in the Bible.* San Diego: Lura Media, 1988, p. 5.

Trible, p. 12.

ourselves and that inner belief was destroyed by another.

The problem with being misunderstood is that we don't have the ability to change another's perception of us or of a particular incident. What's done is done, and often our feeble attempts at making it right or justifying ourselves only serve to dig the hole deeper. While we should make an effort to clear up the misunderstanding, the problem escalates when we demand to be understood. As tough as it seems, there comes a time that, when we have spoken the truth, we must let go of the outcome.

Following that thread a bit further, we find as we mature in faith that there are times when we must let go of a resentment or an accusation, not just when we've hit a brick wall, but willingly. When do ideas such as sacrifice, submission, participation in the sufferings of Christ, and death to self, need to be used? As a woman living long before the advent of Jesus, Hagar may have had no conception of those themes. We, however, live in the light of the New Testament, and there might come a time when we choose to remain on the margins, being misunderstood and even maligned, in order that God's purposes be fulfilled, and in order that something of great value may be birthed in us or in another.

The word *martyr* has become tied up with the co–dependency and victim vocabulary, and pop psychology warns us of the danger of being a martyr to another. Yet Jesus held up martyrdom: "Greater love has no one than this: to lay down one's life for one's friends" (John 15:13, *NIV 2011*). Very few of us will be asked to take a literal bullet for a friend, but we may have to willingly suffer misunderstanding, gossip or punishment, even when we've done little or nothing to deserve it. I must admit that I hate that. I want my reputation to be clear. I'm willing to accept responsibility for what I've done (usually), but I am so unwilling to take upon myself what I do not deserve. It's not fair. But sometimes, that is exactly what I have to do, like it or not. It's what Hagar should perhaps have done.

You Will Pay

Then Sarai dealt harshly with her.

See, Hagar. You should have kept your head down and your mouth closed. Now look what you've got. The Hebrew word used in this passage as affliction, or harsh treatment, is the same verb used to describe the sufferings of the Hebrews in Egypt during the time of Moses. Hagar may have been forced to perform hard labor, or perhaps Sarah took a whip to Hagar's back to teach the insolent slave–girl a lesson she would never forget. Whatever Sarah did, I don't think it resulted in a quiet discussion between the two women, for it brought Hagar to the point of no return.

When I ask myself why Sarah would be so mean–spirited toward Hagar, I realize a couple of things. First is that this may simply have been the culture of the day. Life was hard for a slave, and this may have been the expected treatment for the slightest of infractions, real or supposed. In a slave economy, there were always eyes watching from the shadows, and if one slave got away with stepping over a line, others might draw courage from their actions and try the same thing. So it was vital from the owner's perspective to make sure each knew his or her place—and stayed there.

A second possibility is that Sarah may have been facing her own share of desperation. Hagar was getting uppity, tossing her weight around, and Abraham was withdrawing, unwilling to rescue Sarah and take the lead. Sarah could have been terrified that she would lose her status, that Hagar would replace her in Abraham's eyes, that she would never have a child, and that this fanciful promise from God was just a pipedream. She likely feared her own failure and her inability to reproduce. Fear can be a tremendous motivator but rarely leads beyond self–serving behaviors.

The other factor at play relates to the dynamics that had been brewing between the two women for more than 10 years. It is likely that Abraham obtained Hagar when he had taken his people to Egypt. Genesis 12 tells us that because Sarah was a beautiful woman, Abraham was afraid that the Egyptians would kill him and take her. So in order to protect his own life, Abraham instructed Sarah to claim that she was his sister. Because Sarah was functioning as a wife to the Pharaoh, Abraham was looked on favorably by the Pharaoh, and, in the bargain, accumulated male and female servants, probably including Hagar.

So here we have two women. The first, Sarah, was sacrificed to the Pharaoh's bed to protect Abraham, and he was made more prosperous because of her involvement with the Pharaoh. The second woman, Hagar, was then used sexually by Abraham and Sarah to get what they wanted, namely a child. When Sarah looked at Hagar, a slave from Egypt, did she remember with shame the high price she had paid in those early days? If so, as we peel back one more layer of the story, we find a convoluted triangle of sexual energy, shame, and betrayal. Perhaps it was out of the depths of her own shame that Sarah raised her hand to Hagar.

Have you ever been treated harshly? Perhaps it was within the context of your relationship with a man, where words or fists have made their mark upon you. You may have been the target of the neighborhood bully, who had no mercy for younger and weaker children. Or your harsh treatment may have been experienced in the Bible study you cherished, when lies were spread about your character (as a matter of prayer, of course), and sisters in the Lord suddenly ostracized you rather than taking the time to find out the truth.

Linda was the president of a group of home–school parents. She confided in another mother about her experience as a teenager dabbling in witchcraft. Within days, she was asked to step down from what she loved because of her "questionable moral character." As she sobbed in my office, I recognized Hagar in her tears and understood a bit more how we hurt each other.

Harsh treatment can also occur on the job. While physical abuse in the workplace is generally a thing of the past, it has been replaced with more subtle actions that can be just as damaging. Whispers, innuendos, sexual harassment, and withholding of information can all do their work. At times this treatment comes from fellow employees; at other times, from the boss who wants to keep employees "in their place" or to manipulate them into resigning. It's called a hostile work environment, and it stinks, but workers find themselves trapped, grateful to still have a job.

Many employers don't even bother to make the workplace difficult for an unwanted employee—they simply take their cue from Donald Trump and say, "You're fired." It's standard procedure now, as the word is given and the ex–employee is escorted from the premises. Another employee will pack up your personal items to ship to you. No good–byes, no engraved watch, no closure, just a "don't let the door hit you on your way out." Ten, twenty, thirty years gone in an instant. Seldom is there recourse. The company has spoken to the lawyer first.

The message is the same, whether from Sarah's whip or "Donald Trump's" mouth. *You have no value. You will pay, whether it was your fault or not. You are done.* We must come to grips with what is true, whether we lost our job or suffered abuse because of our actions or because of circumstances beyond our control. It is helpful to get perspective from other people so that we don't blame ourselves for something beyond our control or excuse ourselves when we have a lesson to learn from our actions.

Sadly, people in the church are not exempt from harsh treatment. In this scene, Sarah and Abraham stand as symbols of what goes wrong. There are many abuse issues within the church, subtle and blatant: power struggles, disregard, sexual harassment and abuse, toxic faith concerns, and blindness toward domestic violence. Many have experienced the abandonment of Abraham when the hierarchy, the church, and the men (and women) we trust to protect us won't—and don't. Sarah can be male or female, who all too often deals harshly with another under the auspices of the church of Christ. It is a great sorrow, but sinful intent and sinful actions do occur in the church just as they do in our broader culture.

I wanted to stop here because there is a righteousness in exposing sin in another and in recognizing the plight of the victim. However, we must not leave this subject without considering whether we have been guilty of meting out our own harsh treatment. The old story line is true all too often: the husband gets chastised at work and comes home and yells at his wife. The wife then screams at the children, the kids kick the dog—and pity the cat that lives in that home. The scenario is a twist on the teachings of Jesus in Matthew 18. A servant owed his lord money, begged to be forgiven, and he was. Then he turned around and refused the same forgiveness to his fellow servant.

I must ask myself, "Who am I treating harshly?" Oh, it may not be with a whip, but we use other punishing tools. Gossip, sarcasm (literally, flesh–eating words), isolation, emotional abuse—all become Sarah's whip in our hands when the power differential is in our favor (and even sometimes when it's not). Whenever I am in the boss–husband–wife–child–dog cycle, I must be willing to make the effort to break it.

Why do we act like this toward each other? Do we treat someone else harshly simply because we have the ability to do so? Are we more likely to have cruel words for our spouse or child if we were chastised at work today? And if we are the recipient of brutal treatment, how do we survive? When we turn the other cheek and that one is slapped as well, what do we do then? Hagar made her choice.

I'm Outta Here

And Hagar ran away from Sarai

I want to stand up and cheer Hagar on, congratulating her for her courage, but the more cautious part of me wonders how she could have dared to run away. After all, a slave was property, and a runaway slave could have been pursued, captured, beaten, and returned to her mistress—or even killed. If she thought that Sarah had been harsh before, who knows what might await her if she were caught. Yes, the consequences for Hagar's escape could have been difficult for her to bear.

What could she have been thinking, endangering herself and her unborn child in such a way? We're not talking about a walk to the corner store here. No, if Hagar was on her way to Egypt, she had a long, difficult journey ahead of her through treacherous desert. She could easily have become dehydrated and died, especially if troubled by morning sickness. And even a nomadic people used to traveling did so in groups; no one went off alone. The odds of Hagar arriving safely at her destination are not in her favor.

So why would Hagar run away? Probably the same reasons we run away. We're impetuous and we fail to count the cost of our choices, or we are so desperate that we see no other options. Either I leave or I will die. It is of no consequence if I die in my escape because death would be better than what I face here.

Hagar's story reminds me of the story of another woman who felt the same compulsion. Harriet Ross Tubman described her intention: "I had reasoned dis out in my mind; there was one of two things I had a right to, liberty, or death; if I could not have one, I would have de oder; for no man should take me alive; I should fight for my liberty as long as my strength lasted, and when de time came for me to go, de Lord would let dem take me."[7]

I have to write about the first of these reactions, the impulsive decision, from the role of observer because the cautious streak in me definitely

---

[7] Marcia Y. Riggs, ed., *Can I Get a Witness?: Prophetic Religious Voices of African American Women : An Anthology* [Paperback]. Maryknoll, NY: Orbis Books, 1997, p. 27.

holds me back—I am not known to be impetuous. But I know some people who are. They decide quickly and many times end up regretting that spur-of-the-moment choice. These tend to be "out-of-the-frying-pan-into-the-fire" people. They manage to extricate themselves from a terrible situation but quickly become embroiled in another that ends up looking an awful lot like their previous one. Impetuous, rash—we all know people like that. Maybe you are one of them.

But I know the pain involved in being the other kind of person, the one who weighs every decision closely and who has lost many an opportunity because she was waiting for one more bit of information, a fourth or fifth confirmation from God so she can be sure not to make a mistake. She is terrific at investigating options but struggles to commit, to decide for sure. I sat in the coffee shop with a dear friend, lamenting my lot in life and my hope that things would change. After patiently hearing me out, she said, "I have only one word for you." She took a marker out of her purse, and wrote boldly on a napkin, MOVE. She understood that my indecision was paralyzing me. It didn't matter so much which way I moved but that I did something, anything, to combat the inertia I was experiencing.

The obvious answer here is balance. There can be strength in being decisive and wisdom in being cautious. If we know we are impetuous by nature, then we need to check with at least one or two trusted friends before making any major life decisions. "She who hesitates is lost" should not be a wall-hanging in our living room. If we are at the other end of the continuum, we need to understand that we cannot always choose perfectly. There will be times when we simply must trust ourselves enough (and trust God enough) to give it our best shot.

I'm not sure that Hagar's decision was made because of an impulsive nature. The words *and Hagar ran away from Sarai* send chills up my spine. I think Hagar was desperate, and her action has a familiar scent. I've been there, and it's quite possible you've been there. *I can't take it anymore.* It really doesn't matter what "it" is—a screaming infant, an oppressive spouse, chronic illness, a job that challenges my integrity daily—"it" is simply too much. If something doesn't give, we feel like we will go crazy, hurt somebody, or hurt ourselves.

Are there times when running away is the wisest choice? Absolutely. The problem is that when we need to make that decision, we may do so from a place of deficit (depression, fury, exhaustion) so that our process is flawed. That is why we must have a framework from which to see clearly.

- *What are the dangers of leaving?*
- *What am I leaving behind?*
- *What do I need to resolve in my own heart and mind before I go?*
- *What might it look like if I have to return?*
- *What do I need to learn?*

There are ways to run away that leave us physically in the circumstances that are difficult but emotionally thousands of miles away. We disconnect. We build layer upon layer of protection (pounds, a prickly personality, emotional deadness) that keep us from feeling the pain of our situation. We're still there, day after day, but our emotional suitcases are packed and waiting on the porch. Sometimes it seems the only alternative we have, but it is a hollow way of living, and one day we wake up and realize that there is no one at home in our heart—all that had been alive in us has slowly died. We can turn back, but it is a long and painful journey.

A healthier option is a time-limited "running away"—finding some way of separating from the difficult circumstances for a time of decision or recovery. It may be as simple as a weekend by ourselves at a friend's cabin or a few days at a retreat center. Or perhaps we need to ask a friend to take the baby for a few hours so that we can sit by the water and pray. In the case of marriage, there are instances when a therapeutic separation can be helpful, but if the goal is saving the marriage, then there must be a reunification plan in place.

As soon as I suggest these possibilities, I feel the guilt train barreling down the tracks. *How could I selfishly think of getting away for a few days when my family needs me, my job needs me, my spouse needs me?* Although there are a number of pat answers to the guilt-train way of thinking, the real answer is to stop buying tickets for it. We do not need to feel guilty about taking care of ourselves or about choosing life over a slow death.

In the end, we may decide, as Hagar did, that we must run. Annie Dillard knows the feeling: "You can't test courage cautiously, so I ran hard and waved my arms hard, happy."[8] If run away we must, then we must run hard, run strong, run well.

[8] Annie Dillard, *An American Childhood.* New York: Harper and Row, 1987, p. 108.

Heading Home

... she ran away from her.

Hagar runs, but where? Where does a pregnant slave run when she is escaping from her owner? Where does a wife run when she is leaving an abusive spouse? Where do we go when we've suffered the abuse of a power–hungry pastor? Where can we go?

Hagar decides to head home. We can surmise her direction and destination because Shur, where she stopped to drink water, was between Abraham's tent and Egypt. It is likely that it had been 10 years since Hagar had been in Egypt, so whatever home she knew could have changed drastically, but because it was all she knew, in her desperation, she fled toward home.

Actually, heading home when we are a mess is not such a bad idea. Now I don't necessarily mean home to mommy and daddy, for that is not always a healthy choice. Rather, it is a returning to a place, a person, or a situation where we belonged. When we have stood up to Goliath (I Samuel 17), or run from Jezebel (I Kings 19), we search for protection, a place where we can collapse and not have to be brave any longer.

We run to the stability of home. The house I call home has stood on the same street, in the same neighborhood of the same small city in western New York for more than 50 years. My parents built it themselves, and we have pictures of them holding me as a newborn, even before the sheetrock was on all the walls. I've lived in 13 houses since then and created many homes for my own family, but home will always be that house on Klinger Ave. It has withstood the rigors of Buffalo winters and even my dad's aborted attempt to burn it down when he forgot that he was cooking bacon. It is my place of origin and it is home to me.

We run to the comforts of home—the grilled cheese sandwiches and tomato soup, the memories of a simpler way of life. There were a lot of comforts in that home. Band–aids®, hot chocolate after sledding, the warmth of the fireplace on a frigid day, and the cool water of the pool on a muggy summer night all were a part of my growing–up years. My mother is now in her mid–80s, but she still cooks when I go home, and I find comfort in being provided for in that simple way. On days when I am weary and discouraged, I long to be comforted. I wish I could run somewhere and be held as I cry, pouring out all my sorrows and fears in the comfort of another's love for me.

We run to the safety of home. Life with Sarah was proving to be dangerous to Hagar, and home held the promise of safety, even as unlikely as that promise might have been. There was a wide, hot desert between Hagar and home, but she could see past the desert to what seemed like comparable safety. After all, could the desert be any worse than what she was experiencing?

Poet and writer Erica Jong found a way to run home by changing roles, and while she didn't turn back to her childhood home, she did turn to the traditional character of wife to escape:

> Even when I was forty–seven, full of my own power, my own identity, something in me wanted to escape from the fray and dwindle into a wife. It seemed so comfy, so safe. I was so tired of fighting. I drifted through the days, sleeping and shopping. I did not want to carry on the war.[9]

What we realize is that stability, comfort, and safety are what we long for when we have run away, but sometimes, we end up running to an illusion of home. Maybe we've never truly known the stability of place or person that we could trust. Perhaps the comforts of home are imaginary, and the safety we longed for is non–existent. Hagar had only two frameworks from which to choose: Egypt and Abraham/Sarah. She now knew what Abraham's tent signified, and for her, the fantasy of what might be in Egypt was better than what she knew in Canaan.

A folk song asks a pointed question: "O sinner man, where you gonna run to?" One version suggests that he run to the rock, to the river, and to the sun, but none of these places holds the answer he is seeking. I wonder what it is that we run to? What are the alternatives we choose in search of comfort? You can name the list, and you can also name your "drug" of choice. We all have something.

---

[9] Erica Jong, *Fear of Fifty*. New York: Harper Spotlight, 1995, p. 228.

Running home, we may encounter safety, comfort and stability, or we may find that our judgment has been flawed. Yet there is another way to run home, and that is to run as David did, to run home to what we know, even if we're clinging to it by our fingernails. We can run to the convictions of our faith, to the bottom line of who God is to us, even to the lap of our Heavenly Father. Psalm 61 *(NIV,* 2011) is a good example:

> From the ends of the earth I call to you,
> I call as my heart grows faint;
> lead me to the rock that is higher than I.
> For you have been my refuge,
> a strong tower against the foe.
> I long to dwell in your tent forever
> and take refuge in the shelter of your wings.

Running to our convictions requires intention, the willingness to stop before we run off impulsively—so we can remember the vows we have made, the grounding we have had in our faith, and the character of God himself. Not too long ago, after a prickly encounter with someone at the office, I found myself up to my neck in self–pity. Oh, I felt so bad for myself that I bought my favorite ice cream cone—a double–dip chocolate pecan—on the way home. About two hours later, I suddenly realized that in all my pity–partying, I had failed to even think about going to God.

Yet even when that happens, God still manages to get our attention, for our God is one who searches for the lost lamb and calls his children home. Nineteenth–century hymn writer Will Lamartine Thompson gives voice to the invitation of Jesus: "Come home, come home, ye who are weary, come home."[10] William P. Young, author of *The Shack*, expresses it in today's language: "You know, that place where there is just you alone, or maybe God, if you believe in Him. Of course, God might be there, even if you *don't* believe in Him. That would be just like Him. He hasn't been called the Grand Interferer for nothing."[11]

---

[10] Will Lamartine Thompson, *The Song Book of The Salvation Army.* Verona, NJ: The Salvation Army National Headquarters, 1987, #264.
[11] William P. Young, *The Shack.* Newbury Park, CA: Windblown Media, 2007, p. 12.

Sometimes we run away with no intention of seeking God, and discover that God himself finds us, just as he found Hagar. At other times, God may just be doing the nudging, inviting us into parts unknown so that he can get our attention, just as he did for Mack in Young's book. But we're getting ahead of the story. For first the path toward home leads Hagar through the desert.

Thirsty

by a spring of water in the wilderness ...

When you're running, sooner or later, you are bound to get thirsty. And so it was that Hagar needed to stop and rest, and she did so at the spring on the way to Shur. When we are most desperate, we do need to run—not to escape from our circumstances forever—but to find the spring where we honestly acknowledge our thirst and begin to drink in what we need.

Sometimes, it is our own persistent thirst that forces us to stop even though we've become proficient at running on fumes for quite some time. Sooner or later, we discover that we are not a magical pink rabbit that never runs out of energy. There comes a time when we cannot take another step. We are done, finished. We elbow Elijah out of the way and claim our space under the broom tree (I Kings 19).

We may not even notice how thirsty we are until we stop. Like a long–distance runner, we've concentrated so much on the mechanics of the race that we don't recognize our own thirst or the dehydration that comes from lack of fluids. I've been there spiritually. The ministry was consuming, the children were demanding, my husband needed me, and I was growing thirstier by the day but not recognizing it. I was dried out and didn't even know it.

We had spent nearly six years in poorly funded and understaffed inner–city ministry assignments. I sat in the chapel one Sunday evening as friends had come to fill the pulpit for us. They sang from the Scriptures, "He who began a good work in you will be faithful to complete it ... he who started the work will be faithful to complete it in you" (based on Phil. 1:6). I sat with tears coursing down my face, convinced they were simply wrong, and that there was no way God could complete anything in me. I was exhausted and defeated and couldn't see any way out. I had to stop and recognize the truth of our circumstances and how dehydrated I really was. I'd made the mistake that M. Craig Barnes warns of: getting used to living in the dry places.[12]

---

[12] M. Craig Barnes, *Sacred Thirst: Meeting God in the Desert of Our Longings.* Grand Rapids, Mich.: Zondervan, 2001.

What I needed was a change in assignment, because I had gotten too far into the desert to get out on my own. However, in our system of appointment, the expectation is that we wait for the denomination's leadership to make that change. When my husband and I had to make that request, it felt like running away from work we had been called to do. Yet in facing the truth of my situation and admitting my need, I was able to find a refreshing spring to drink from.

Annie Johnson Flint described those times in words from her reassuring hymn:

> When we have exhausted our store of endurance,
> When our strength has failed ere the day is half done,
> When we reach the end of our hoarded resources,
> Our Father's full giving is only begun.[13]

The physical symptoms that signal the lack of fluid are not immediate and strong, but they have great impact. As our bodies become less nourished, we become less effective in our work or athletic activity and encounter a weariness that is difficult to shake. Tears dry up and our eyes become sunken. If unchecked, dehydration can lead to liver damage and even death. It's fascinating that the physical symptoms resemble the spiritual warning signs that appear when we are dry and parched. Our work bears little fruit, we are weary of well–doing, and little things move us to tears. We're living out a slow death of the spirit and don't even know it.

We can't ignore the symbolism of Hagar's story. She encounters God (God makes himself known to Hagar) when she stops by the stream and finally admits that she is thirsty. As long as we are running, there is no space for God. As long as we are so full of self and full of our own resources, there is no room for a thirst for God.

As Hagar found, thirst can be identified and then satisfied. The psalmist described an admission of thirst:

> As the deer pants for streams of water,
> So my soul pants for you, my God.

[13] Annie Johnson Flint, *The Song Book of The Salvation Army*, #579.

My soul thirsts for God, for the living God.
Where can I go and meet with God?
—*Psalm 42:1–2* (NIV 2011)

The psalmist identified the thirst, but it was Isaiah who best articulated the invitation. "Come, all you who are thirsty, come to the waters … " (Is. 55:1, *NIV 2011).* When speaking to the woman at the well, Jesus told us more: "Everyone who drinks this water will be thirsty again, but those who drink the water I give them will never thirst. Indeed, the water I give them will become in them a spring of water welling up to eternal life" (John 4:13–14, *TNIV).*

Go to the well, my Samaritan sister. Follow the path of the panting deer, descendant of David. Bend down to the spring, Hagar. Don't ignore your thirsty lips, your thirsty heart. Drink greedily, take in great gulps, because God is waiting. Are you thirsty? Drink deeply, because God is waiting.

Lost and Found

The angel of the Lord found her …

Thus begins the interaction between God and Hagar. Picture Hagar as she hungrily drinks the water at the stream. So many desperate thoughts must be racing through her head. *I'm so exhausted and frightened. Will I make it any farther across the desert, or should I turn around and return to my mistress? Did Sarah send the other servants to track me down? Will Abraham change his mind and come after me, knowing I'm carrying his son in my womb?* Hagar may have even dozed off by the stream, drained as she was by her journey. Still desperate, Hagar paused, and as she waited, these glorious words came to be: *the angel of the Lord found her.*

Most families have a story or two about young children running away and being found again. The children may have been upset when they've run away, but usually by the time they are discovered, they're just happy to be found. Part of that joy comes from knowing that someone (often many people) cared enough to look for them. In Hagar's story, she may have thought that the only one who might possibly look for her was the slave assigned to follow her tracks and drag her back to Sarah. Yet here was this strange presence who found her—yes, her, Hagar, only a slave woman.

In Hagar's experiences, we see glimpses of the story that will continue to unfold throughout the Bible. Here is a God who sought and found a frightened woman. Over and over, the message comes through the Word of God: I will find you, I will be with you, I will not leave you. Jesus painted the picture of the Good Shepherd, who had 99 lambs accounted for but went out in search of the one missing lamb (Luke 15). It is a powerful image of God who is not content for us simply to wander on our own towards him but diligently seeks after those of us who are "missing in action."

Jesus said it himself in his conversation with a wealthy tax collector named Zacchaeus: "For the Son of Man came to seek and to save what was lost" (Luke 19:10). It's interesting to note that this often–quoted verse does not talk about someone who would have described himself as lost. While the religious people labeled him a sinner, Zacchaeus had a house of his own, money and a powerful position—he had the goods. Jesus looked at him and saw his "lostness," just as the angel of the Lord recognized the lostness in the wandering Hagar. There is a lost little girl or little boy within each of us, and Jesus longs to find us. I love these words written by Jill Briscoe, a woman who has spent many years in ministry: "If you've lost heart, Jesus knows where you lost it. He loves to find lost things—like lambs, coins, sons—anything precious that has been lost in the heat of battle. He has been here: hay in his hair, dust on his feet, splinters in his fingers, pain in his eyes."[14]

A famous poem by Frances Thompson explores the image of God as the Hound of Heaven. What kind of dog best images the way God seeks after you? For a bit of fun, try these out. A graceful golden retriever, a loyal sheepdog, a nipping chihuahua, a hypervigilant guard dog, or a plodding bassett hound? Is the dog that is nipping at your heels more like Lassie or Scooby-Doo? And are you ready to turn and let the Hound of Heaven find you?

[14] Jill Briscoe, Focus on the Family Newsletter, date unknown.

Hagar, Slave of Sarah

And he [the angel of the Lord] said,
Hagar, servant of Sarai ...

As Hagar would soon find out, the God who seeks and finds is also the God who stays involved with His people. When the messenger of God speaks, he does two things. He names Hagar, and he defines her by the role she fills in the household of Abraham.

The angel of the Lord knew her name. That is so encouraging to me. God knew the name of an Egyptian slave–woman. God knows the name of every child that was killed in the typhoon, tsunami, and earthquake and every child who wanders the streets of Calcutta begging for food. He knows my name and your name. And He knows the names of the unnamed, those the narrator doesn't identify throughout the Bible, such as the Levite's concubine, the woman at the well, and the widow who gave her last cents in the temple. Each one has a name known to God.

He also defines Hagar by the role she fills in society. Even though Hagar has run away, she has not escaped who she is. She is still Sarah's slave, even if she now is a runaway slave. The angel could have called her Abraham's wife (or concubine), but he did not. Instead, he reminded her of the identity that is at the root of the conflict and struggle in her life. Running away doesn't change that fact.

We are also known by the role we fill in society. We label ourselves by how we introduce ourselves to others. *Hi, I'm JoAnn Shade, Daniel's mother*, or *Welcome, I'm JoAnn Shade, the pastor of this church.* The angel's naming of Hagar in this way does not necessarily mean that the messenger was reminding Hagar of her place. Hagar knew her role all too well. Perhaps it was God's way of letting her know that he knew her—not only by her name but also by what she has been through.

At times I get frustrated when I am known only for the role I fill or the skill I bring to a given situation. I am a competent pianist, and in many gatherings I am asked to provide the accompaniment for the singing. I love to play the piano and find great joy in doing so, but at times I wonder, *Can you see me beyond the keys of the piano? Just one time, invite me to preach or teach, to write a song or to share my story.* I want others to see beyond the outward, obvious skill to the rest of me. We are multi–dimensional; we are much more than only a mother or father, only a wife or husband, only an administrative assistant or middle manager.

Hagar too was more than a slave. Hagar's pregnancy was the opportunity for her to add to her resumé. Yes, she was the slave of Sarai, but by the end of her interaction with the Lord, she also was known as the mother of Ishmael, as the mother to a great multitude of descendants, and as a woman who both saw and named God. She became far more than a slave–woman, both in the eyes of God and in her own eyes.

Beyond that kind of knowing, there is more. For Hagar, it was being seen for the woman she could become: a woman who would name God, a woman of courage, and a woman of obedience. I love watching young girls—8, 9, and 10—before the seismic waves of adolescence hit. They are so full of potential, and it is fun to dream about who they will become. I have one young friend who is sure to be a politician; another will be a diva of some kind. A third will likely have an impact on cancer research. I can see their possibilities, and if they can survive the throes of the teenage years in contemporary society, they will be something to watch for sure.

This interaction with the angel reminds us that we do not need to remain where we began, either with God or with each other. A friend who had gone through a difficult divorce recently said to me, "I'm tired of people talking about 'single moms' as though that characteristic defines the person. Yes, my husband walked out on me, but it didn't change who I was. I am so much more than just a 'single mom.'" God definitely sees beyond the labels and calls us out of our circumscribed way of thinking into a new way of looking at ourselves and our circumstances.

There's one more layer in God's knowing of Hagar, for I believe that he saw her heart. He knew her for who she truly was. He saw her as a woman who was fearful but who also could desperately love and, ultimately, who could look to God in faith. I wonder who God sees when he looks at me, at you? Whatever ability, potential, or soul he sees, there is a smile of delight on his lips (Zeph. 3:17). As my friend reminds me from time to time, if God has a refrigerator, my picture is on it—and so is yours!

Beyond the specific words used by the angel of the Lord, the underlying power of his words is that they were spoken. God speaks to Hagar! All too often, we think that God speaks only to those who fit the mold, who are saintly and upstanding citizens. This passage proves that theory wrong. "Hagar, slave of Sarai" was spoken out loud. God's messenger (or perhaps God himself[15]) actually appeared to a slave–girl and spoke to her. Just as God spoke to Abraham and Moses, God spoke to Hagar. And just as God spoke to Hagar, we too can hear and be responsive to his voice.

In the end, when God calls, we must be in a place where we can hear and respond. The old song comes to mind, "When he calls me, I will answer, I'll be somewhere listening for my name." Whether we stop at the spring and drink, acknowledging our spiritual thirst, or deliberately silence the many voices that clamor for our attention, we can hear the one Voice that speaks our name. For God has something to say to us, something that he wants us to hear.

[15] Gunkel raises the question as to whether this was an angel or Yahweh himself. "Older versions introduced Yahweh himself in such cases; later editors and copyists were offended by the notion of Yahweh's being too intimately involved with the world and preferred to speak of Yahweh's angel in these passages—that is, an inferior divine being." (Hermann Gunkel, K.C. Hanson, eds., *Water for a Thirsty Land: Israelite Literature and Tradition.* Minneapolis: Fortress Press, 2001, pp. 71–72).

Where Have You Been?

Where have you come from?

This seems to be a question with an agenda. When my son comes home late, I ask him, "Where have you been?" I want to know who his companions have been and whether he's gotten into trouble. When I've been gone all afternoon, my husband might ask, "Where have you been?" He wants to know the answer to that question, but he also wants to know how much money I've spent. "Where have you been?" seems to be one of those layered questions that asks for more than appears on the surface. "Where have you been, Hagar?" becomes "What happened that you had to leave? What's going on? Why did you feel you had no other choice?"

Not only is it a question with an agenda, but it is also an arresting question, for it caused Hagar to stop her flight. She was forced to consider where she had been and, potentially, what had brought her to the Negev desert. If her flight was a spur–of–the–moment running, the verbalized question gave her permission to stop and to consider changing direction.

Why is it that when God asks us questions, it seems as though he already knows the answer? He uses that tactic quite a bit. God asked Adam, "Where are you?" when Adam was hiding in the garden (Gen. 3). He asked Elijah, "What are you doing here?" at the cave at Mount Horeb (I Kings 19). And Jesus asked Mary, "Why are you weeping?" at the empty tomb (John 20). It would appear that in each situation, God knew the answer to the question.

As a parent, I've been known to do the same thing, usually for two reasons. I want my children to tell me the truth about what they have done and how they are feeling and to consider the implications of the question. When God asks questions of his people, it is because the questions matter in the spiritual health of the individual (or of the community, such as in some of the prophetic literature). His questions allow us to see and articulate the truth about who we are, what we've done, and the emotions we are experiencing. We can consider how our history and identity have brought us to where we are today and how they influence the choices facing us each day.

As Hagar was forced to consider this first question, "Where have you come from?" it was with an opportunity to look back and reflect on her history. *From the land of Egypt, from the tent of Abraham, and from the tyranny of Sarah, that's where I've come from.* For Hagar, the question allowed her to admit that she was a woman with an Egyptian heritage. What did that mean to her? Was she proud of her ancestry or was she ashamed? Did she weep for her separation from mother, father, and siblings? Or had she enjoyed the adventure of new places as she traveled with Abraham's household?

Where have you come from? *I've been in Abraham's tent.* Oh, Hagar, I am so sorry. To be forced to go into a man's tent and to accept his seed as you did is something no woman should have to bear. Even if there was some sense of cultural prestige in it, it was still an offense against your body and soul. No woman, no person should be so disrespected. You indeed were a victim of birth and circumstance.

That is Hagar's story, but the question can be for us as well. When it is spoken, it takes us back to the question of identity, when we can name our history in such a way as to see the hand of God along our path. Indeed, where have you been? Think of the homes you've lived in, the churches you've attended, and the jobs you've held. Name a place or two where you found warmth, and the people who made you smile or shared your faith experience. Who hurt you? When were you lost? Who called your name? Consider the impact of times of great joy or times when you were frightened and unable to move.

An additional way to answer the question, "Where have you been?" is to mark the spiritual path we've traveled. A favorite book of mine is Hannah Hurnard's *Hinds Feet on High Places,*[16] the journey of Much Afraid as she attempts to reach the high places. Much Afraid finds herself with crooked feet and mouth, but she learns she is not alone in the journey. She is accompanied by Sorrow and Suffering, and the Chief Shepherd in the high places meets her when she most needs him.

Have you been to the desert, to the mountaintop, to the garden of

[16] Hannah Hurnard, *Hinds Feet on High Places.* Uhricksville, OH: Barbour Books, 2000.

Gethsemane? What are the high places you have sought? Who have been your companions? Can you map out, as John Bunyan did, the trough of despair,[17] or can you remember the dark night of the soul as named by St. John of the Cross?[18] Can you see the hand of God along your path? Do you have, fixed in your memory, stones of remembrance that are symbolic of times and places of spiritual challenge? The stained–glass windows in the sanctuary, the choir loft on Christmas Eve, a tree in the woods at a camp in midwinter, the hardwood floor of my living room in Shaker Heights, and the ocean at daybreak are all on my story line. From time to time, I pause to retrace my steps, so that when the messenger of God asks the question, I am ready with the answer.

[7] John Bunyan, *A Pilgrim's Progress.* Oxford: Oxford Press, 1966.

[8] John of the Cross, "The Dark Night of the Soul," from *Collected Works* translated by Kieran Kavannaugh and Otilio Rodriguez. Washington, D.C.; Institute of Carmelite Studies.

Now Where Do You Think You're Going?

... and where are you going?

Yes, Hagar, where are you going? Usually, when I get in the car, I know where I am going: to work, seminary, the grocery store, or the coffee shop. I know how to get there, what I'm going to do when I arrive, approximately how long I will stay, and what I hope to accomplish while I'm there. Once in a while, I will leave my house without a destination in mind, but usually with a reason to go. I might be upset with someone, confused about something that has happened, or, as in an old airline commercial suggested, I just might need to get away.

In considering the intent of the Lord's two questions to Hagar, I wonder—if he asked the first to help Hagar face what had brought her to this place, verbalizing an answer both she and the Lord knew already, why did he ask the second? It may have been with a similar, yet distinct, purpose that would enable Hagar to own her confusion and sort out what she was trying to do. Or did the angel simply want to show her that she really didn't know where she was going?

By asking the question, did the Lord allow Hagar to look ahead to what could happen if she stayed on the path she had chosen? By stopping, catching her breath, and contemplating the possibilities, Hagar could see that both she and the child she was carrying could die in the desert. Are we looking at the grace of God? Some of us are relatively sensitive to the leading of God and make reasonably good choices over time. But others are like my friend, who explains: *I am so hard-headed that I can only see one alternative at a time. It is as though God has to hit me "upside my head" to get my attention, but when he does, then all my energy goes into following the path he has revealed.*

Our denomination is one that changes the placement of its pastors by way of a phone call that indicates they are "under farewell orders." I've experienced as much as a weeklong gap between that initial phone call and the follow–up call that says, "This is where you're being assigned." In recent years, that time gap has been shortened considerably, but even a few hours of wondering about the new location is nerve–wracking. *Where will it be? Will I like it? Will the people like me? Will there be a Starbucks?* Just tell me where I'm going, and I can make peace with that, but don't leave me hanging without an answer.

Most of us, however, don't have our destination proscribed quite as clearly. We face major decisions about where to go to college, whom to marry, what house to rent, and what job to take, as well as the daily challenges of how we spread out our time.

Where are you going? The huge popularity of Rick Warren's book, *The Purpose–Driven Life*, stands as evidence that ordinary people are as interested in this question as are political leaders, college athletes, and aspiring Miss America candidates. We wonder about our path in life in ways that go beyond location. We wonder about where we are going, and also about who we are becoming along that journey.

As a therapist, I learned that my work was less about providing answers to my clients and more about helping them to ask the right questions. In fact, biblical counselor Larry Crabb suggests that the role of a counselor is to ask the tough questions that produce confusion, and he warned about the danger of wanting to wrap the painful questions in pretty paper.[19]

In the early days of my work, I often turned to my notebook of resources that contained a section on questions.

- How do you feel about that?
- What is important to you about this experience
- Can you talk more about this?
- What was it like growing up in your home?
- How do you see yourself in the future?
- What are your strengths and weaknesses?
- How did you achieve that?
- How did you act when things were better?

---

[19] Larry Crabb, radio interview, undated.

- What are your hopes for counseling?
- What is overwhelming you?
- Where is God in this for you?

So, where are you going, sister or brother of Hagar? Do you know in what direction you're headed? Do you have a destination in mind? Is it even attainable, or does it have all of the dangers of a desert? Is there a dream at the end of that road that you are living for? Is it time to switch gears or turn around? Here is a good time to pause at the spring in the desert and let the questions have a chance to be heard. Don't be in a rush to find answers; they will come when you give the questions some room.

Answering the Questions

... and where are you going?

On my son's first day as a freshman, I risked my life in the high school parking lot to pick up my 15–year–old. As a good mother, I wanted to check on his day at the new school building. "Did you have a good day?" His monosyllabic answer grunted affirmatively. "Did you see any of your friends?" "Mom, what is this, '20 Questions'?"

I wonder if Hagar thought she was playing 20 Questions in her exchange with the messenger of the Lord. It is revealing that she, like my son, answered the first *(where have you come from?)* but not the second question *(where are you going?)*. Does Hagar tell us something about herself in her failure to respond? She apparently knew that what she had left was unbearable and that she needed to get away from Sarah. But beyond that, she may have been clueless as to where she was going.

Hear my take on your story, Hagar. My guess is that you were very brave and very determined because you escaped from what you couldn't tolerate anymore. Your courage was most likely mixed with a sense of desperation, for you may have felt that you had no other choice than to run. But after the initial surge of courage, did you doubt your decision? I do that too. Should I keep going? Should I go back? I don't know what to do. Maybe that's why you didn't answer the second question of the messenger—because in the end, you really didn't know. You knew what you were running away from, but you had no idea what you were running toward.

Somehow, Hagar, I'm beginning to understand that it's OK not to know all the answers. It's OK to recognize the great paradoxes, the contradictory messages about life and about God when all the pieces don't fit together as well as I would like. When I demand that all the contradictions be explained, then I am demanding to control my world and not accepting the sovereignty (in–charge–ness) of God. Going down this path leads me to the ugly truth about myself—I want to be in charge. I want to know what's happening. I want it all to make sense. And I want all this NOW!

Sometimes, though, we come to the point where we can say, "I don' know." I don't know where I'm going, I don't know what is happenin or why, and I won't demand to know. I am willing to accept the myster of faith and the belief that God is in control and that he is good. I don' know if you were thinking about any of this, or if you were just running but sometimes God uses the times when we are most desperate to revea something profound about himself and about our relationship to him.

An old prayer meeting chorus asks this question: "What will you answer be?" For a time, "I don't know" is an honest answer. But soone or later, we must answer in a way that reflects the direction of our heart Either I desire to move toward God or I am moving away from him We can choose to say: *I am becoming a person of God, a woman or a ma who is passionate for Jesus. This is who I am. This is where I'm going.*

I am a map person. I want to get the Trip–Tik® from AAA and follov the lines on the paper to my destination. Switching to the GPS that m husband got for Christmas has been tough on me as I struggle to trus the voice coming out of a little box on the dashboard. With the GPS no longer see the full picture, and I don't even know the annoying voic that is talking me through my trip. It's definitely a paradigm shift fror tracing out the route in advance on the map in my hands to trustin the one who enters the destination and the unknown voice who guide at every turn. Hagar's narrative continues to remind me that I can trus the One who sees the destination and who allows his voice to be know by those he loves.

Did He Really Say That?

Return to your mistress and submit to her.

Did the angel of the Lord really tell Hagar to return to Sarah and submit to her? How could he do that? His message doesn't fit my image of a loving God. I don't want to hear this. When my young sons didn't want to hear my voice, they would cover their ears, close their eyes and sing their own nonsense song as loud as they could. And that's what I want to do. I want to blot this mandate out of Hagar's story. I want to pretend that God knew how painful this was for Hagar, that he loved her and had a wonderful plan for her life, and that his plan did not include Sarah. But God had another way, as is so often the case.

What do we do with this direction? We suck it up, is what we do. There are times when God's direction to us is to return and submit, and if that is clearly what God is revealing to us, we must do it. Now I'm not in any way suggesting this is a command to abused women to return to their abusive spouses, for God is clear in Malachi: "For I hate divorce, says the Lord, the God of Israel, and [I hate] covering one's garment with violence, says the Lord of hosts" (Mal. 2:16). A husband is to love his wife as Christ loved the church and as much as he loves his own body (Eph. 5:25, 28). Nor is this counsel to remain in other abusive situations where sin is rampant and a person is in danger.

Unlike Hagar's encounter, we usually don't get such direct intervention and direction in our lives, so must depend upon wisdom and discernment in hearing the leading of God. Counsel can come from many directions, and over time we will find clarity in the way we should go.

What I am talking about is the kind of submission that God requires when we've thoughtfully and prayerfully sorted out God's direction and aren't quite thrilled with where that may lead. We know that God has spoken, but all we want to do is to lie in the middle of the floor and pitch a fit or head to the corner and pout, because his direction just doesn't fit in with our preconceived ideas about the rest of our lives.

Submission to God's direction is a biblical concept we simply cannot ignore. We must look at submission within relationships in light of the overarching principle of Galatians 3:28 *(there is now neither male nor female, for you are all one in Christ)*, and the overarching principle of mutuality of submission of Ephesians 5:22 *(submit to one another out of reverence for Christ)*. We must also understand that Jesus is in the business of changing hearts. Still, this kind of direction forces us to trust God in ways that we may have never done before. We trust that the voice is clear and that God has a purpose in his direction to us. Even so, some are challenged to submit, as was Hagar, while others are challenged to do battle against an oppressive system (the Hebrew midwives—see Exodus 1).

My recent ministry experience is an example of this tension. We are itinerant in our relationship to our denomination, which means that when our denominational leaders tell us it is time to be reassigned, we are reassigned. One of those calls came at a time when, for the sake of our teenage son, we felt strongly—no, we knew—that we could not go at that time. While I saw our decision as one that moved toward our son, there were those who suggested that we were running away from the call of God. I've loved my ministry but began to dream of what life might be like in a different venue. I began to feel a freedom that was refreshing and life–giving as we prepared to move in a different direction.

Then the angel said, "Go back." Another door was opening for us to remain in the denomination and also to provide stability for our son. The glimpse of "freedom" was enticing, but when I was willing to stop by the spring, to wait and to listen, the Lord spoke. "Go back … submit," and that is what I needed to do at that time.

My "go back" story has unfolded with some remarkable opportunity. Because I returned in obedience, I've been in position to bring light to darkness and comfort to others from the comfort God has promised and given to me. It hasn't always been an easy return, and I've had my share of anger and frustration. But now, looking back on those days and on what has happened since, I am, with Habakkuk, "utterly amazed." My inclination was to demand to know why the Lord said, "Go back," but that was the chapter that I could not read until it was time. I had to rest in the knowledge that God's promise to be with me would be enough.

One hunch about Hagar's story is that the angel's words to her were a way of protecting the baby she was carrying. Perhaps Hagar could have withstood the trip to Egypt, but a newly pregnant woman traveling alone in the desert would be risking her child's life. Might it be that she needed to swallow her pride and return to the relative safety of Abraham's tent so that her child could be safely brought to delivery?

It is also possible that God wanted to work in both Hagar's and Sarah's lives. Sometimes he places us in situations that stretch us in powerful ways as we must learn to cope with and to work with someone who is very different from us. Not only did Hagar need to hear the Lord, but Sarah did as well. With God's intervention in Hagar's life, the balance will change when she returns to Sarah. She will tell her story, and Abraham will name the boy as the Lord has said. Sarah will have to look on from her own barrenness, knowing that Hagar has now been acknowledged as the mother of many.

When I am in the midst of the confusion that occurs when I can't comprehend God's plan, I must stop and recognize that God knows the whole story. While I am like the proverbial blind man trying to identify the elephant by touching only a leg or trunk, God sees and knows the whole elephant. This is one of the rich lessons of Hagar, that the meta-narrative—the big story—is in God's hands, not my hands.

Yes, it would have been more to my liking if the angel had freed Hagar from the bonds that connected her to Sarah and to Abraham, but that wasn't her story. The angel really did tell Hagar to return and submit. He did not explain why this was the chosen plan. Instead, he balanced his seemingly difficult words of submission by showing himself to Hagar and giving her a sacred promise. For Hagar, that was enough.

A Promise

The angel of the Lord also said to her,
"I will so greatly multiply your offspring that
they cannot be counted for multitude."
And the angel of the Lord said to her,
"Now you have conceived and shall bear a son;
you shall call him Ishmael [God hears],
for the Lord has given heed to your affliction."

You will have a son. There they are, the words of the desert promise made to Hagar, the promise that allowed her to return. Had the message stopped at the first command, "return," it is possible that Hagar would have done so, since the words came from the Lord, but she may have done so with resentment or confusion. Yet here comes God with this glorious promise to Hagar, both of the upcoming birth and the long-term consequences of her obedience.

Without a trumpet fanfare or a public relations consultant, God announces. The Bible reports other annunciation narratives (announcement stories), such as Manoah's wife (Samson, Judges 13), Zechariah (John the Baptist, Luke 1) and Mary (Jesus, Luke 1). These announcements told of the imminent birth but also named the child, revealed its gender, described the ways the child was to be raised, and indicated something about his purpose in life. Such was the case with Hagar as well. Not only was she told that she would have a son, but she was also given his name, Ishmael, a name that would be a constant reminder that God knew what she was going through.

Hagar was also told that her descendants would be too numerous to count, an echo of the promise given to Abraham (Gen. 15:5). Now in our world where population control is a political issue in many developing countries and where women can control the number of children they have based on their ability to raise them, the idea of numerous descendants is a foreign concept. But in Hagar's time, descendants were a sign of power and success, a status symbol of sorts, but also an economic necessity. Descendants meant military might and economi stability—in short, descendants meant survival.

We will break into the flow of Hagar's story for a moment to conside the structure of the words Hagar was given. "Return … and I will … This pattern of a command linked to a promise runs through the page of the Bible, from Genesis to Revelation. Here are some examples:

- God to Noah: If you build an ark … I will establish my covenant with you. (Gen. 6)
- God to Moses: If you lead … I will bring you into the land of promise. (Ex. 6)
- God to Abigail: If you do what is right … I will protect you. (I Sam. 25)
- God to David: If you commit your way to the Lord … I will make your righteousness shine like the sun. (Ps. 37: 5–6)
- God to Solomon: If my people who are called by my name humble themselves, pray, seek my face, and turn from their wicked ways, then I will hear from heaven, and will forgive their sin and heal their land. (II Chron. 7:14)
- Jesus to his followers: If you abide in me … then you will bea much fruit. (John 15)
- God (through Paul) to the Philippians: If you pray … then th peace of God will guard your hearts. (Phil. 4:6–7)
- God to the seven churches: If you conquer … I will keep you from the hour of trial, and I will give you the tree of life, the crown of life, a new name, the hidden manna, authority, white robes, a place on his throne. (Rev. 2–3)

I'm glad that God is up–front about his expectations for his peopl We live in a society where telemarketers can promise us the world, fre of charge—well, with only a small shipping and handling charge—an then ask, "May I have your credit card number, please?" And before w know it, our credit card is maxed out because of that "free" offer. Bu the Lord makes no pie–in–the–sky promises in his dealings with Haga The Lord is straightforward: if you do this, I will then respond, not i the prosperity gospel sense, but in the care of a Father for his children.

An old hymn by Fanny Crosby provides us with our final glimpse of the workings of God. “Only a step, only a step. Come, he waits for thee.”[20] Even in the context of the grace of God, both rich and free, there is an if/then condition. As in the story of the lost son (Luke 15), God waits for us to take the step toward him. This I will do, says the Lord.

Even when the response from God has come, we are still left with the responsibility to receive what he is providing. Relationship with God is not as simple as the if/then factor in a science experiment or a 10th–grade geometry proposition. There is a continuing obedience and giving, a continuing provision and receiving. I have a friend whose mantra is “the Lord will provide,” but when that provision comes in the form of an outstretched hand from a neighbor, he fails to see that as the Lord’s work and is unable to receive what is offered to him.

As she listened to the messenger of the Lord, Hagar was willing to trust God for the future, knowing that her “if,” responded to in obedience, would allow God to fulfill his promises to her. But there is one more component to this annunciation story—that of the identity of the boy she was carrying.

Fanny Crosby, *The Song Book of The Salvation Army*, #255.

Description or Prescription?

He shall be a wild ass of a man ...

What kind of promise was this? Oh, I understand the "many descendants" part, but the words used to describe the son Hagar was carrying sound more like a curse than a promise. Is there any way to look at them in a positive light? I'm not sure that these words would have been reassuring to Hagar. They definitely wouldn't have been something for me to look forward to.

First, were the words of the angel a description of who Ishmael would be, such as "He'll have his father's red hair and blue eyes," or were they predicting and prescribing that this is how he would turn out? Was this simply an acknowledgement of the genetic heritage Ishmael would own and the personality that he was born with, or was it a foreshadowing of the development of Islam hundreds of years later? Was God saying: "With my foreknowledge, this is who I see him to be," or was his message, "This is how I've made him, this is my plan for him?"

Without getting too complicated, this is similar to the debate about predestination. Simply put, some people believe that God has foreordained the path that each person will take and that God has chosen ahead of time those who will come to faith and those who won't believe. There are other people who think that each person ultimately has a choice (or many choices) as to what path to follow and can choose a life of faith or a life of disbelief. In this view, God may know the outcome of each path but the individual can choose what path to take. So in the same sense, God may have been saying to Hagar, "This is how it will be and you can't do anything about it," or God may have been saying, "Ishmael is going to have these characteristics, but he will choose what to do with them."

I'll borrow from one wiser in the explanation of Scripture and more knowledgeable of the original language to sort out what this may mean. J. Gerald Janzen says that the statement, "He will be a wild ass of a man" is a good thing because Hagar would recognize it as representing the freedom of the wilderness. "If he enjoys his freedom by living (tenting) in the wilderness, it is because, even while she returns to dwell in Canaan, the freedom of the wilderness goes with her in that middle power she has learned by the spring of water"[21] Because his mother had been willing to return and submit to Sarah, in contrast, her son would one day live in freedom. The statement also could indicate that he has the ability to survive in the wilderness, so that even if he has to leave his family for whatever reason, he is also able to survive without them.

The freedom described by the angel's words had to be a relief to Hagar. As a slave, Hagar might have assumed that her son would be bound by slavery as well—what a curse for a strong-willed child! This boy, says the Lord, will live outside the boundaries of his birth. As a "wild ass" of a man, he will not be domesticated, but rather will be able to survive in the wilderness.

Even if there are possibly some positive implications for the initial description, the words that follow are troubling. "His hand with [or against] everyone and everyone's hand with [or against] him, and he will dwell in the presence of all his brethren." While Ishmael may grow up to become a free man (unlike his slave mother) and a strong man, he will not be mistaken for a nice man.

Here's the question for modern-day parents. Was Ishmael a child who was flawed or marked from the start? Did he ever have a chance to be at peace with his brother? Is that kind of destiny a possibility for our own children? No doubt that they have distinctive personalities from birth, and some children are born with handicaps that will limit their movement or attainment in life. What does that mean for their future?

These are difficult questions that I don't feel prepared to answer, other than with this response. God is powerful and he is good. He has provided a path of redemption for all people, slave or free, wild or mild, withdrawn or friendly. In Christ, personality flaws can be redeemed and embraced. In Christ, children like Ishmael can be loved and accepted. They may struggle with anger or a need for wide-open space, but they too can find an experience of salvation and the gift of grace.

---

[21] J. Gerald Janzen, "Hagar in Paul's Eyes and in the Eyes of Yahweh (Genesis 16): A Study in Horizons," in *Horizons in Biblical Theology* (Vol. 13, No. 1: 1991), p. 13.

You See!

You are El–roi [the God who sees]

Hagar names God. What a powerful name she chooses: El–Roi, the God who sees! When the Lord named Ishmael, he taught Hagar that "God hears." Now Hagar confirms the Lord's presence with this description, for indeed, Hagar has been seen and has been known by God.

That, at least on some days, is a scary thought. The possibility that the Lord of the universe is something of a celestial Santa Claus, "making a list and checking it twice," can be cause for discomfort.

In talking with a friend about our experience in counseling, I blurted out, "It seems as though my therapist has seen me naked." Now, let's be perfectly clear: this is a metaphor; I remained fully clothed during my counseling sessions. However, I was vulnerable enough to him to feel as though I were fully exposed. Initially, that seemed like a shameful experience, and at times it was. He saw through me, through my defenses, my excuses, and my blame–shifting. As in the sacrament of confession, I named my sin in his presence. He "saw" me, and he knew me.

Yet there was a goodness in those hours as well. First, because it eliminated the need for game–playing and the wearing of masks. I didn't need to cover up in his presence. The amazing part was that even when he saw me "stripped" of the protective layers that had kept me safe (and isolated), he didn't reject me. This then allowed me to be seen for who I truly am. I discovered a new joy in being female, an appreciation for my strengths, an awareness of my weaknesses, and a better understanding of where I was most vulnerable to sin.

While any human interaction is an imperfect example, I believe it is how God saw Hagar and sees us. God knows where we've been and where we may be planning to go. God knows the pain we've suffered and the pain we've inflicted. He sees our mixed motives, our baby steps of faith, and the deepest longings of our hearts. He sees us as we are and embraces us, but he also sees us as we can be and invites us to that vision of wholeness.

Elizabeth Reynolds Turnage asks why it is that the despised and rejected seem more likely to see and be seen by God. She suggests that it may be that they are "shameless in their shame; that is, they are exposed, and thus they no longer have anything to hide."[22] When our feelings are raw, when we have no resources of our own, we are not hampered by the layers of pretense that separate us from God. "Here I am, God—what you see is what you get."

Because Hagar named God, we too can name God. We can begin with the name given to God in the Scriptures. He is self-described as Yahweh, "I am who I am," a name that was so holy to the people of Israel that they refused to speak it out loud. The book of Job describes God as El-Shaddai, the almighty God, with the connotation of fruitfulness. Adonai is translated as "the Lord," while the word Jehovah (Yahweh) is often teamed with a modifier, such as Jehovah Jireh (the Lord will provide) and Jehovah Rapha (the Lord who heals). Scripture also uses metaphors to name God, such as strong tower, shepherd, rock, father, mother, light, and breath.

We are not limited to the names and images that we know, for we can also find our own names for God that are consistent with what we know of his character. One that has been significant to me in recent weeks is Basket Weaver. Now I don't know that there is a specific reference to God as basket weaver in the Scriptures, but consider the possibilities. God is a creator—in fact, *the* Creator—and we sing with the children, "He's got the whole world in his hands." Isaiah tells us that "a bruised reed he will not break" (Is. 42:3), and the basket weaver is known for handling the fragile reed with care. Life can be understood as a weaving, and the hand of God can be seen in the patient weaving together of our lives. Baskets are even named, sometimes after their weaver, and are containers, often with specific purposes. Just as the biblical metaphor of the potter and clay carries with it very precious implications, so too does the concept of the basket weaver.

Our names for God can change over time, just we might change our name for our mothers. As a midlife woman, I no longer call my mother "mommy" or "mama" because our relationship has changed

[22] Elizabeth Reynolds Turnage, "Questions for the Desperate" from "Views from the Edge" series. Mars Hill Graduate School. www.mhgs.edu.

from infant/caregiver to adult daughter/adult mother. We too can use the varied names of God as they fit our life circumstances. When we need a shepherd, we are comforted by the rod and staff. When we need a mother, we can rest in the shadow of God's wings. When we are overwhelmed, Jehovah is our strength.

I'm excited that Hagar was able to name God, and that her name for the Lord was preserved for us through history. But I'm also glad that we too can use various names and images of God in order to deepen our belief and find new and holy ways to connect with the Almighty God.

Thus ends the Genesis 16 account of Hagar, slave of Sarah, concubine of Abraham, and namer of God.

where have you come from, Hagar?

out of Egypt, my sister
slavery's chains your solemn companion
your body to edge into the patriarch's tent
a captive, restrained

never your own, my sister
with legs forced to spread for Abram's seed
your womb to harbor another's hope
a vessel, invaded

labor on, my sister
with hands to soothe another's brow
your back to sustain the stripes of envy
a vassal, afflicted

run away, my sister
the wilderness promises a reverent rendezvous
your lips to taste of the spring's refreshment
a vision, encountered

jas

hagar

margin–dweller
a stranger's presence
your eyes observe an alien land
beware

son–bearer
a matriarch's surrogate,
your womb bursts with Ishmael's strength
deliver

desert–wanderer
a cast–off concubine
your tears salt the Beer–lahai–roi well
drink

God–namer
a blessed woman
your voice unveils a seeing deity
speak

jas

Going Back

Hagar bore Abram a son ...

Following the encounter with the Lord, Hagar returned to the tent of Sarah and to the household of Abraham. Did she slink back in fear? Was she filled with shame? Did she grieve the departure of the angel and dread the return to "same–old, same–old," or did she enter the tent with her head held high, full of her experience of God? It's possible that Hagar knew all these feelings. How could she have gone back?

Begin with fear. Think of an occasion when you had to walk into a room knowing you were to be reprimanded, maybe even beaten (fired, expelled, tongue–lashed). By the time we get to such a place, we're all worked up about what might happen. We've envisioned the worst–case scenario. Our palms are sweaty, and our heart is beating at twice its normal rate. Sarah had already treated Hagar harshly before; she will hardly listen to the story of an angel who appeared to a slave–woman. If she did, what would Sarah's reaction be? Would it threaten the promised son? Would Sarah stake her claim to the baby and discard Hagar after his birth?

Hagar may also have had to battle shame as she returned to Sarah. After all, if she left believing that she could survive on her own, it was a humiliation to return because she needed once again the sustenance of the Abraham family tent. I've been in a few of those, "I–told–you–so" situations, in which my best intentions and efforts bombed. As with fear and anxiety, the anticipation can be much worse than the actual response.

My guess, however, is that Hagar's encounter with God changed her in a number of ways. I attended the funeral of a well–respected Christian woman, who had left an incredible impact upon hundreds of young people, both in her work as a principal and in her presence in the church for more than 50 years. If it was said once, it was said 10 times: When I'd be discouraged, ready to give up, Mrs. Jackson would say to me, "Dry your tears, hold your head up, put your shoulders back, stand up tall." Now I'm not sure that Hagar had a Gloria Jackson to speak those words to her, but having held her own with a messenger of the Lord himself, this was a different woman returning to Sarah.

Ultimately, Hagar was able to retrace her steps and walk back into that tent because she had the assurance from the Lord that this was what she needed to do. What a difference that makes! When I reflect on my ministry, I realize there's no way I could have done even half of what I've accomplished if I hadn't been convinced of the Lord's direction. That assurance didn't take away all the anxiety, nor did it remove the uncomfortable aspects of my work, but it allowed me to say, "This is what I am meant to do."

Sometimes we have to go back. We have to eat crow, apologize, forgive. We find ourselves walking up to our Sarah, looking her in the eyes, extending our hand. We can do so in a way that simply "grins and bears it," making the best of a terrible situation, yet remain filled with resentment and bitterness. Or we can take the high road, claiming the scriptural injunction to love enemies and to pray for those who persecute us (Matt. 5:44). Choosing that road means we are willing to put love in action, to not repay evil for evil, and to follow the instruction of Romans 12:18: "… as far as it depends on [us], live at peace with everyone," even our own "Sarah."

As I was writing these words, I received an e–mail from a friend asking for prayer covering during a time of spiritual struggle. She wrote:

> I am longing for God to free me from bitterness toward one particular person. We have a long history, and I've been wounded pretty badly by her, both in the past and even now. I've attempted to talk with her about the situations that have caused injury to my family and myself and have felt as though we've been able to work things out, but then she does something that causes the bitterness to rise again. Please pray that I will be freed from all bitterness and that I won't speak to others about the unkind things just to make myself feel better.

I am believing for my friend today, that God will be gracious, and that El–roi, the God who sees, will know both her pain and her intention. And I believe that this too is Hagar's prayer toward Sarah, a prayer of a woman redeemed by the presence of the Lord.

Giving Birth

Hagar bore Abram a son.

Upon her return to the tents of Abraham and Sarah, Hagar watched her body expand and her waistline disappear as her pregnancy progressed, until the day when she actually went into labor. I remember those days of waiting, when every twinge had me wondering if this was to be the day. I had the perspective gleaned form natural childbirth classes, but it is likely that Hagar's only instruction in birthing a baby came from the other slaves. While childbirth was an accepted part of the life cycle, it was more dangerous in Hagar's day, and she certainly had no guarantee that she would survive it—well, except for that promise of the angel.

I wonder what Hagar was thinking and feeling during the waning days of her pregnancy. Was she frightened, excited, or worried about giving birth? Did she wonder if Sarah would claim the child once he was born and banish Hagar—or possibly sell her to another owner? Would Hagar be able to see her son grow to adulthood? And how would she manage, knowing Sarah's unpredictability?

Yet the time came. I love the words of Luke's account of the birth of Jesus: "And the time came that she should be delivered." In the same way, Hagar's time came, and one day, her muscles began to liberate this promised son. I can remember, somewhat, those long hours of birthing. There is a blessing in that the memories of birth are hazy, for it is definitely painful, with or without Dr. Lamaze. Yet it is pain with a purpose, with the promise that at the end, there will be a child, the promised one.

I've given birth to three sons as well as lost two babies in early pregnancy. But for me the concept of birthing isn't reserved for babies. I've birthed music, poems, essays, and books. I've birthed lots of ministry program concepts, and a vibrant new ministry facility. I've had a hand in birthing new life in others and offering the gift of hope to many. At times, I feel like Rebekah (Gen. 25:22), jostled by what is growing in my metaphorical "womb." "You've got a lot percolating," mused a friend recently.

What is longing to be birthed in you? It may be a masterpiece of art or a small kindness, a new friendship, or a ministry to migrant children. It may simply and profoundly be that the image of Jesus is being created within you. Whatever it may be, it is yours to nurture and release, not to hoard or squirrel away.

For we have a role in bringing to life and light what is straining to be birthed within us. Renita Weems sees it: "The moment comes when you have to decide for yourself who you are and what your own desires and fantasies are. You also have to figure out what it will take to turn your fantasies into reality and whether you've got what it takes."[23] She lays down the challenge: "Take responsibility for your own growth. God expects you to share with God in midwifing your own wholeness."[24]And so we wait, breathing deeply, in the pain and trust of birthing, with both a faith-filled abandonment to the God of new life and an active cooperation in our own laboring.

> Only God could say what this new spirit
>   gradually forming within you will be.
> Give our Lord the benefit of believing
>   that his hand is leading you
>   and accept the anxiety of
>   feeling yourself in suspense and incomplete.[25]
>
> —*Pierre Teilhard deChardin*

---

[23] Renita J. Weems, *What Matters Most.* W. Bloomfield, MI: Walk Worthy Press, 2004, p. 13.

[24] Renita J. Weems, *Showing Mary: How Women Can Share Prayers, Wisdom, and the Blessings of God.* New York: Warner Books, 2002, p. 6.

[25] Pierre Teilhard deChardin quoted at www.angelfire.com/ultra/yministry.dechardin

A Midwife Comes Alongside

Hagar bore ...

In doing some creative writing about the Christmas story, I invented the character of a midwife at the birth of Jesus. It makes perfect sense to me that Mary didn't give birth to Jesus by herself, and it was highly unlikely that Joseph was her only companion in the stable. The innkeeper would have sent someone running for the neighborhood midwife to come alongside Mary in her labor. During my moment of panic at my son Daniel's birth, I was grateful for my midwife, who could take my hand and say, "Take a deep breath, JoAnn. I am here to be with you. I know that you are struggling right now, but your baby will soon be born." Or, as Julian of Norwich reminds us, "All will be well." Yes, I trust that Mary had a midwife with her and that Hagar did as well.

Male readers, be patient here. You may have those who come alongside you, but there is something about midwife imagery that speaks particularly to women. When we are with child, on the verge of giving birth to new ideas or life choices, or hitting the wall at the height of our pain, we need a midwife, one who is simply "with women." Do you have one or two? My current midwives are a varied lot. One simply props me up when I'm a wreck by feeding me chocolate and hope. Another is this incredible courage–giver who will not let me give up. A third midwife asks the awkward questions that I want to avoid but must hear. And a fourth makes me laugh when I start to take myself too seriously.

What will your midwife do? She's there, you know, to do what you need her to do. She can support you physically, let you know what to expect (she's walked this road before), encourage you to keep going, be an advocate for your choices, and simply hold your hand. She will lend you her strength when you've hit the wall. She will lead the celebration when the baby is born, when the book is published, when your new business opens. She will live out the definition of the word midwife—"with woman."

There may come a time when she will have to take drastic measures to save your life. I love the way Kaye Gibbons describes the birth of one of her characters:

> After thirty–six hours of work with little result, my grandmother decided she would labor standing, holding onto the bedpost for support, letting gravity do what it would. Sophia, however, persuaded her to be quilled, and so a measure of red pepper was blown up my grandmother's nose through the end of a feather freshly plucked from one of her many peacocks. My grandmother fell into a sneezing frenzy, and when she recovered enough to slap Sophia, she did. Sophia slapped her back, earning both my grandmother's respect and an extra dollar. Within the hour, my mother was born.[26]

Makes me wonder which one of my midwife friends would pluck a peacock's feather to save me? And what I would do to save the life of another?

A wonderful midwife friend, especially gifted in wisdom, speaks to what is coming with these words: speed, ease, comfort and joy. They are words of promise and reassurance for all our birthings. Speed, that the labor will pass quickly; ease, that the birth passage will be without obstacles; comfort, that a soothing in distress will be ours by the hand of one who loves us; and joy, that what we have birthed will bring delight to us, to others and to the heart of God. Push on, my sisters!

---

[26] Kaye Gibbons, *Charms for the Easy Life.* New York: J.P. Putnam's Sons, 1989, p. 3.

for a midwife: four haikus

breathe deeply, woman
mine the reservoir of strength
in jagged rhythm

labor on, sister
empower your straining womb,
befriend its aching

let it birth, dear one
deliver up your riches,
liberate promise

bare your breast, mother
let down the life–giving stream,
milk to satisfy.

jas

Who Is This Strong-Willed Child?

And Abram named his son, whom Hagar bore, Ishmael.

Now this is a subject I can write on with experience. Move over, Dr. Dobson—I can write the book on this one, for I had a strong–willed child right out of the starting gate—my firstborn. At least Hagar had ample warning from the Lord—I simply gave birth to mine. Please understand, I love my son fiercely, but he has known his own mind from day one, and mothering him has definitely been a challenge. I must admit that this may be genetic predisposition for firstborns in our family, for my mother tells me that I share many qualities with my son.

In Hagar's case, we don't even know if she had any involvement with the boy once he was weaned, as he may have been raised in Abraham's tent, separated from Hagar. However, she may have been given second–wife status when she returned to Sarah and served in the role of mother as Ishmael was growing up. We just don't know. So instead of discussing the parenting skills needed to raise a strong–willed child, we'll focus on what it means to have a strong–willed child, especially for Hagar. What does having a child like this do to the mother? How does it challenge and change her?

The simple answer to that question—we don't know—is based upon the text. But we can make some assumptions, at least from a contemporary, Western perspective. The first is that parenting Ishmael required Hagar to dig deep within for strength. Parenting is about keeping at it. It is about being consistent, setting limits, and providing a safe environment for the child to discover his own place in the world

A second assumption is that she was in for some battles. It's likely that Ishmael's behavior was unpredictable and would have given Hagar some definite challenges. I watched a friend struggle through this battle scenario when her teenage sons became involved in a gang. She would set limits; they would break them. She would arrange for consequences;

they would thumb their noses at her. How long do you fight for your children? When do you draw the line so that they can no longer destroy the rest of the family?

Ishmael's presence in Hagar's life may have also caused her to doubt her own abilities. Most mothers aren't dealing with the kinds of situations that Ishmael gets into. A friend recently told me about her daughter's early years when nearly every day brought some kind of physical confrontation with another child at preschool. What do you do in those kinds of circumstances? There isn't a pill for a 4–year–old who is defiant. For some of our teens, the threat is to have them declared unruly and sent to the detention center. Unfortunately, sometimes this comes as an easy escape from doing the hard work of parenting. I don't quite see Hagar going to Sarah for advice on what to do with Ishmael—fortunately, our culture does provide for many options in sharpening our parenting abilities and defining our parenting values. Here again, we don't have to go it alone, as Hagar most likely had to.

A final challenge for the Hagar of our mind's eye is that of power. Being Ishmael's mother put Hagar into a triangle of power in which she too often found herself positioned at the weakest angle. Again, we have contemporary similarities such as blended families, in which the step–parent has the least power in the triangle, and the child learns to manipulate the dynamics, often causing unbearable tension in the home. Of course, adults can be manipulative as well, easily falling into the roles of victim, persecutor, or rescuer rather than being able to support each other in the toughest job in the world (parenting).

Kevin Huggins, writing in *Parenting Adolescents*, provides us with challenging words for Hagar and ourselves to conclude this chapter.

> The more a parent is filled with compassion for his teen, the more he wants to get involved with him. Involvement fuels compassion, and compassion fuels greater involvement. And as a parent's involvement increases, so does his influence. Kids tend to watch, follow, and imitate the people who are most involved in their lives … When parents start to get involved in their kids' lives … they begin a process in which God

can ultimately use their lives to transform their kids' lives. The most important rule is to never go back. Never retreat from involvement but always patiently look for opportunities to deepen it.[27]

[27] Kevin Huggins, *Parenting Adolescents*. Colorado Springs: NavPress, 1989, p. 184.

Under Sarah's Eyes

Return to your mistress and submit to her.

I can only imagine what it was like for Hagar to live, day after day, in the shadow of Sarah. Between the birth of Ishmael and the next mention of Hagar in the scriptural account, we can assume that Hagar has returned to a position of submission to Sarah. In those intervening years, much has happened in the meta–narrative. In chapter 17 of Genesis, the covenant of circumcision was established between God and the household of Abraham, so Ishmael, at 13, was circumcised. When the Lord instructed Abraham in this new command, he also gave both Abram and Sarai new names, Abraham and Sarah. With the new covenant and new names came an expanded promise: "I will make you the father of many nations, and I will do so through Sarah," a dubious promise that brought laughter to Abraham's lips. Yet within months, Sarah was pregnant.

These years also brought the visit of three men to the tent of Abraham at Mamre. They again confirmed that Sarah would have a child. This time, it was Sarah who laughed and then lied to the Lord about her reaction (Gen. 18). This appearance of the Lord at Mamre also led to the destruction of Sodom and Gomorrah (Gen. 19).

During this time, Abraham continued in his nomadic lifestyle, wandering in the Negev between Kadesh and Shur, and he also stayed in Gerar. In that town, Abraham again claimed Sarah was his sister, and she was taken into the household of Abimelek, king of Gerar. In explaining his action, he told Sarah, "This is how you can show your love to me: Everywhere we go, say of me, 'He is my brother'" (Gen. 20:13, *TNIV).* When releasing Sarah, Abimilek provided compensation for her, even though he hadn't touched her (Gen. 20:6), and the narrator tells us that Abraham prayed to God, and God healed Abimelek, his wife, and his female slaves so they could have children again, "for the Lord had kept all the women in Abimelek's household from conceiving because of Abraham's wife Sarah" (Gen. 20:17–18, *TNIV).*

Pardon the history lesson, but it sheds some light on what Sarah and Hagar experienced in the years between the birth of Ishmael and the weaning of Isaac, Sarah's son. First, they learned that the Lord was not to be trifled with; he was a God of power and might. Did they witness the destruction of Sodom and Gomorrah, inhaling the stench of sulfur, or did they listen as word of the destruction of Sodom and Gomorrah spread through the tents of Abraham's encampment? However the news came to them, there was one lesson: This was a God to be feared.

Secondly, Sarah had a shameful encounter with the Lord at Mamre. Initially, she was eavesdropping, hearing the pronouncement of the Lord regarding her coming pregnancy and laughing in response (the same response Abraham had had at an earlier encounter). When confronted about her laughter as a sign of her unbelief, she lied to cover up her response: "No, I didn't laugh."

In the Gerar scenario, Sarah faced another situation where she was placed in an awkward situation that potentially put her in harm's way. Yet as a result, Sarah became a very powerful figure; it was because of her that God closed fast all the wombs of the house of Abimelech. Sarah was not a woman to be trifled with either.

The climax for Sarah is reported at the beginning of chapter 21: "The Lord dealt with Sarah as he had said, and the Lord did for Sarah as he had promised." Sarah, after a very long wait, is pregnant! Finally, she has achieved the highest status for a woman in her culture: She will give Abraham an heir.

From a psychological perspective, Sarah's appearance as a demanding woman unwilling to cut any slack for Hagar is a classic reaction to unresolved shame mixed with positional power (Sarah's first–wife status) and personal power (perceived because of what happened at Gerar). Add to that the crowning jewel of her pregnancy, the ultimate sign of her "chosen" status, and Sarah is now unmistakably queen of Abraham's tents.

Perhaps the only consolation for Hagar in this part of the story is that Sarah's reaction did not depend on Hagar's identity or behavior. If it hadn't been Hagar, it would have been someone else. It was enough that Sarah felt threatened. We too may find ourselves faced with a situation in which there is no way to please another. Our "Sarah" can be a person of power in our lives, such as a supervisor, mother or mother–in–law, or caseworker. Onlookers may remind us that if we can't stand the heat, we should get out of the kitchen, but our kitchen door is bolted shut, and we see no way out.

Where is God then? Is there a "way out of no way?" The voices of sisters from the past encourage us to trust God even then. Listen to just a few:

- Edith Schaeffer, 20th century: "Give me strength, Lord, for living this hard moment to Your glory. May I honestly be willing to pay the price that is my part of the whole."[28]
- Margery Kempe, 14th century: "Ah! Lord, for Thy mercy grant me grace to obey and fulfil Thy will, and let never my ... enemies have any power to hinder me from fulfilling Thy will."[29]
- Frances Ridley Havergal, 19th century:

  I could not do without thee,
  I cannot stand alone,
  I have no strength or goodness,
  No wisdom of my own;
  But thou, beloved Saviour,
  Art all in all to me,
  And weakness will be power
  If leaning hard on thee.[30]

Like Hagar, we often find ourselves in situations where there are no options for leaving. We do live in a much different world from Hagar's, and slavery as she experienced it is no longer tolerated in most countries. But there are a variety of situations in which our escape hatch is bolted, yet we understand that God's plan for us is to remain. In a world with a seeming great number of choices, living out that decision can be difficult when our friends wonder why we stay, and they don't quite accept our explanation.

---

[28] Miriam Mindeman, *Songs of a Woman's Soul: A Book of Prayers*. Wheaton, IL: Harold Shaw Publishers, 1998, p. 22
[29] Mindeman, p. 23.
[30] Mindeman, p. 22.

What we know is that "it is what it is." It is possible, though challenging, to live in the tension between what is and what could be, but what is is our "address" at the moment. It's time to be realistic, and praying Reinhold Niebuhr's serenity prayer can give us a valuable framework: "Grant me the serenity to accept those things I cannot change. Give me the courage to change those things I can change. Give me the wisdom to know the difference."

Instead of despairing, we can focus on what is possible. We can learn from our sisters who lived in slavery and find new songs to sing as we go about our daily business. We can develop an inner strength as we discover those resources of our character that are growing daily. We can lean on God, going to him constantly for his provision of courage and power. We can depend on God's people, letting our sisters and brothers lift us up when we need it. We can claim the promises of Scripture, such as the words of Jesus: "And be sure of this: 'I am with you always, even to the end of the age.'"

My favorite example of this kind of focus is found in the film *Shawshank Redemption*. Andy Dufrense is sent to prison for murder, though he is innocent of the crime. Serving his time, he is able to build a library in the prison and help many prisoners gain their high school diplomas. In one powerful scene, though he knows he will pay dearly for his actions, he rigs the P.A. system in the prison and sends beautiful music through the cellblocks. He made the best of each day throughout his imprisonment, but he also worked every night at digging a tunnel through the wall of the prison, and he escaped from its confines after nearly 20 years of stealthy excavation. The movie's tagline describes Andy's outlook: "Fear can hold you prisoner; hope can set you free."[31]

Even when we must submit to circumstances and people that seem determined to bring us to defeat, it is possible to live with integrity, grace, and our own portion of joy. It is likely that Hagar found her sustenance in remembering the voice of God at Beer Lahai Roi and the presence of the Lord at the well. Our consolation is found in the fact that the writer of Genesis is careful to tell us that the well is still there. It is enough to know that when we are on the road that runs between Kadesh and Bered, the well is still there.

[31] *Shawshank Redemption.* http://www.imdb.com/title/tt0111161/quotes

When Envy Strikes

But Sarah saw ...

My friend is getting on a plane to spend a week with a mutual friend, and I am envious. I want what she is going to have: days of laughter, chocolate, heart–to–heart talks, tears, long walks, and courage–giving (yes, she is going to visit one of my midwives, who had the nerve to move hundreds of miles away while I was still involved in "birthing"). I have told my friend that I am envious of her, my rationale being that if I admit it, it will absolve me of any guilt I might feel. This is obviously a silly example because I am definitely happier for her than I am envious, but I do recognize that envy is a terrible curse in relationships. We can be envious of another's house, weight, beauty, family, marriage, career, wealth, or talent. It doesn't even matter if those things are really of more value than what we have—it is the perception of value that causes envy to grow in the heart of another.

What's going on in Hagar's story? Is Sarah envious of Hagar and her son? Is it possible that Hagar's son might even get a portion of the inheritance? Perhaps Sarah is afraid that in a weak moment, Abraham will give it all to this firstborn son. From our perspective, that's unlikely. Sarah was the preferred wife, the first wife, and the promise of the Lord to Abraham was that the covenant would be through Sarah's child. In all likelihood, even if Sarah had done nothing, Isaac would have inherited the majority of his father's riches and his blessing, while Ishmael may have received a small portion out of Abraham's sense of duty to him as a son.

Reading the narrative once again, I am struck by the timing of this battle. Surely Sarah could have thrown Hagar out on the day Isaac was born, but she did not. Perhaps the weaning of Isaac gave Sarah assurance that her son would survive, so now Ishmael becomes expendable. And maybe Hagar had served as nursemaid to Isaac, relieving Sarah of the tedious duty of caring for an infant.

What really happened between Ishmael and Isaac? "But Sarah saw the son of Hagar the Egyptian, whom she had borne to Abraham, playing with her son Isaac" (Gen. 21:9). Picture Isaac at 3 or 4 (just weaned), and Ishmael at 15 or 16. Was there some good–natured teasing or rough–housing?

We've just spent a few days with my sister and her family. My young adult sons enjoyed playing with Lucas and Noah, ages 4 and 2. They tickled, wrestled, and rough–housed a bit with them—good–natured play that Lucas relished and Noah tolerated. That's how boys are, and it's definitely possible to presume from the Genesis text that Ishmael was simply playing with his half–brother. Some translators have assumed an action of mockery on Ishmael's part (the NIV translation say he "was mocking"), although the verb used in other passages is usually translated "play." Was this an interaction between two brothers that was somehow orchestrated into high drama by Sarah's concern for her own son's future?

From the text, we don't even know if Hagar was present when Ishmael and Isaac were together, but it still became her fault; therefore, she and her son would pay. That seems so unfair. Even if Ishmael really did mock Isaac, the punishment is severe. As mothers, we can't be fully responsible for our children's behavior. Of course, if our child bites another at day care, we need to discipline our child appropriately, but we can't stop him from doing it. We don't have that kind of control. That's what makes me think this had little to do with Ishmael's behavior or Hagar's parenting, but instead, Sarah's need to control the future in accordance with what she understood the promise of God to be.

In the end, Sarah never truly sees Hagar as a person, as another woman, but merely as a means to continuing Abraham's bloodline. She used her to give Abraham a son in the past, and now she uses Ishmael's lineage through Hagar as an excuse to preserve her son's inheritance. Ever been used by anybody?

No One's Got My Back

He took bread, and a skin of water, and gave it to Hagar ...

For once, Abraham, would you stand up for this woman? Do you care so little for the mother of your son? Oh, I know that's not how the story goes, for God's meta–narrative required that the line of descendants of Abraham needed to go through Isaac's bloodline, and we must respect Abraham for being obedient to what may have sounded strange, even to him. (We can sympathize with Abraham, as "the matter distressed Abraham greatly," but it was because it concerned his son, not Hagar). But I wish that someone had Hagar's back. Hagar has done what she's been told to do (return and submit), and now it looks like Sarah's gotten in a snit and wants her gone. How dare I want to argue with God about the course of history? But it seems so unfair, after all Hagar has been through already, that no one is watching out for her—or at least that's how it appears.

I have to admit that I'm sensitive to this, because I've seen it so much, both in my ministry in The Salvation Army and in the counseling office. The welfare reform movement is an excellent example. In 1996, changes in federal law promised to end "welfare as we know it" in the United States. I've watched young women do what they've been told to do, even to the extent of trudging through the snow to their work assignments (so they can maintain their food stamps). However, they are now up against a system that has as its goal the lowering of the welfare rolls, not the success of individual recipients. The promised supports in lieu of cash payments exist, but they're getting more difficult to access. The system has gotten more punitive, all too often forcing these women between a rock and a hard place. Is there no one to stand up for them?

Other scenarios come to mind. I've heard too many accounts involving domestic violence when a woman gathers up her courage and finally calls the police, only to encounter unsympathetic law enforcement personnel, problematic laws, and highly paid lawyers who leave her wandering in Hagar's wilderness. She wasn't asking for it, and she didn't provoke the violence, but she had no advocate.

There are also those whose personal stories are cut and pasted from the pages of Cinderella but never manage to get to the Prince Charming part. This Cinderella clone is the one who pleases, the one who works, and the one who is constantly rejected. It is never good enough, which she translates to mean *she* is never good enough, and she comes to believe it to be true (although often it isn't). We shake our heads and wonder, how could a mother treat her daughter like that? But we also have a glimpse of the pain the mother has suffered (just as we can see Sarah's pain). We live in an imperfect world, and life remains unfair.

We have to believe that things are better in the church, and sometimes they are. But not always. We sit in the wrong pew, we step on another's toes, we ask the sensitive question, or we correct the wrong child, and we find the church less than hospitable. We get in a battle with the Christian education director or the head of the women's ministry, and we may be the recipient of the pastor's suggestion that perhaps we'd be more comfortable worshiping somewhere else. It may be that something we've birthed gives offense—a wayward child, a book that raises controversy, or a passionate commitment to a less–than–popular cause—and we find ourselves marginalized even within the church. How good it would feel if someone defended us, but it doesn't happen.

If you're there, if you sense that no one has your back, please know that there are those of us who are sickened by the actions of the Abrahams and Sarahs in your lives. We see what they do. You are not alone in this. While some in the social service field seemingly do have a streak of Sarah and Abraham in them, there are also those who have an overflow of compassion. Godly men and women determined to change laws and attitudes work in emergency rooms and courtrooms. Others share your pain from your family of origin, and good counsel is available so that you won't repeat the cycle. A quiet woman on the fringes of the church is praying for you. Seek out these unnamed sisters and brothers of Hagar in the churches, in the agencies small and large, and in your neighborhoods. Seek until you find, knock until the door is opened. And when you have the strength, you can join that sisterhood or brotherhood; you too can stand in the place of the angels.

Yes, and know too that although it doesn't look like it in this story yet, God *does* have your back. The Almighty doesn't always intervene as we would like (or even demand), and why he does or doesn't remains a mystery. But he is faithful. Sometimes he stops the storm, sometimes he sends an angel (in various guises), and at other times, he simply holds us when we stagger into his lap or collapse by the well. Don't give up—as Hagar is soon to find out, God hasn't forgotten her name.

One more thought. Sisters and brothers, if we're in the position of Sarah or Abraham in the life of another, we have a choice in each encounter. As I say on other pages, we can choose mercy. Yes, maybe she got pregnant without a husband, made some stupid choices (she'll probably admit it), and knows how to manipulate the system. She's got her issues, but we all do, and we can cast some stones or cast her out. But if we are serious about being guided by Jesus, we'll drop our own stones (see John 8 for the story) and use those empty hands to reach toward the Hagars in our lives.

Banished

... and [Abraham] sent her away.

Overnight, Hagar's life changes once again. Last night, at the big celebration, she was the mother of Abraham's heir; this morning she is an outcast, thrown upon the mercies of the desert to live or to die. Who can survive for long with a skin of water and some bread?

I've watched it happen. A phone call, or a hastily called meeting, and her world changes overnight. In the world of ministry, another woman has been stripped of her livelihood, her home, her calling, because her husband has fallen. If she honors her marriage vows, she loses a place in ministry that she cherishes. Or she finds a note, a scribbled phone number, and a trace of lipstick. And while he may be the one to move out, she too is banished from the life she has known, left to struggle financially and emotionally, wondering what she could have done to keep him pure.

Ever been sent away? Banishment's clothing comes in many different colors and sizes, and they are found in the men's department too. The list is posted from basketball and cheerleading try–outs, and your name is missing. Walmart or another big box store comes to town, and the shop that sustained your family for 20 years puts up a "Going Out of Business" sign and hands out pink slips. It happens to parents as well. When schizophrenia attacks their 25–year–old son, their world is turned upside down. The family is devastated, friends don't know what to say, and they're bumped out of "normal" circles.

While the situations vary, there is an eerie similarity to the feelings. While men may immediately react with fury, for banished women, often shame and self–blame are stronger than anger. Reflecting on her experience of betrayal by her clergyman husband, my friend expressed her reaction:

> I recall the words of my pastor husband as he said,
> 'Be quiet and just listen to me! You forced me and you
> are punishing me. You have to make me the villain

to justify your own life. You are so self–righteous.' The seething in his voice haunts me, a seething I had heard before. I was unworthy. I was the one who could not be trusted. The hatred, animosity, and all the justification for his sexual acting out poured out on me. The knot in my stomach that stores all the accusations and the blame began its twisting. Truth began to elude me. I struggled to discern fact from fiction. I felt inadequate and foolish. My world was spinning out of control.

One of my favorite all–time movie scenes is from *Good Will Hunting*. The therapist, played by Robin Williams, works with young Will, who has been struggling with his life story, thinking that he was to blame for how his life had turned out. Williams, in a moment that turned out to be self–revelatory as well, grabs Will (Matt Damon) and screams, "It's not your fault!"

Feel the anger, Hagar. Let the sorrow wash over you. Admit your fear. Accept whatever responsibility you must for your circumstances. But don't wallow in shame and self–remorse. "It's not your fault!"

Although Paul's words were written to the Corinthians long after Hagar faced her banishment, they do provide us with a thread of hope, even in the midst of banishment: "We are hard pressed on every side, but not crushed; persecuted, but not abandoned; struck down, but not destroyed" (II Cor. 4:8, *TNIV).* Hold on, Hagar. Hold on, my sister. Your story is not over.

Desperation

... sent her away

What do you do when you are desperate? Ever been there? Oh, I could put on my church–woman face and tell you that the first thing I do is kneel by my bed and pray. Yes ma'am, my first reaction is to run to Jesus. I've been walking with the Lord for many years, but I've got to admit that when the terror of desperation strikes, I cave. It may be tears, a nasty word or more, or a quick flip though my list of the top 10 strategies to deal with crisis, but seldom is my first reaction to turn to God. It's a hard reminder that when the going gets tough, we tend to kick into our default mode, and more often than not, our default setting is despair, chaos, or ultra–control, not dependence on God.

I get the sense that Hagar was reacting out of that kind of desperation. She was in the middle of the desert; the only water she had was gone; the sun was beating down on her; and she could see no way out. God had left her responsible for this promised son, and now she knew that she and her son were going to die. So much for the assurance of God that he would have many descendants—this was the end of the line.

Where's this reaction coming from? This is from a woman who had seen God, who even named him as "the God who sees." Hagar and Almighty God were on a first–name basis. Yet she still couldn't see beyond the immediacy of her situation. Been there, done that? Somehow we (the church, evangelicalism) have painted the picture that Christians can't be desperate, or if they are, they can't say it out loud to anyone. They have to look as though they are in control, even in the midst of horrific circumstances.

Turn, however, to the Psalms. There are many psalms of lament, but one powerful one is Psalm 88 *(TNIV)*. Read these selected verses:

> Lord, you are the God who saves me;
>   day and night I cry out to you.
> May my prayer come before you;

turn your ear to my cry.
I am overwhelmed with troubles
and my life draws near to death.
I am counted among those who go down to the pit;
I am like one without strength....

Your wrath lies heavily on me;
you have overwhelmed me with all your waves.
You have taken from me my closest friends,
and have made me repulsive to them.
I am confined and cannot escape;
my eyes are dim with grief.

Sure looks like the psalmist knew something about desperation.

Catherine of Genoa, recognized as one of the saints in the history of women in the Church, was willing to be honest before God about her experience of desolation:

> O Lord, what would you have me do further in this world? I neither see nor hear, nor eat nor sleep. I do not know what I do or what I say. I feel as though I were a dead thing. There is no creature that understands me. I find myself lonely, unknown, poor, naked, strange and different from the rest of the world.[32]

Sojourner Truth said it bluntly: "O God, you know how much I am distressed, for I have told you again and again. Now, God, help me."[33]

As a teenager, I watched as my pastor experienced the sudden death of his wife. Week after week, he would stand in the pulpit and open the Word of God, and week after week he would break down in sobs before he reached the end of his sermon. At 15, I really didn't know what to do with this blatant display of sorrow, but apparently the denominational leaders were disturbed enough by it that he was soon replaced—at least that was my perception through teenage eyes. Of course, I don't

[32] Mindeman, p. 91
[33] Mindeman, p. 104.

now the full story, for he may have requested a change himself, but he impression I got was that it was not appropriate for a man to be so verwhelmed by grief.

I hate hearing these words at a funeral: "Look how well she's holding p." But that's what we do. Particularly in the middle–class evangelical ulture, we've been trained to keep our emotions under control lest we e seen as less than spiritual. At a recent memorial service, I watched the hildren of a beloved 89–year–old matriarch dab at a tear or two, while he grandchildren sobbed in their grief. While some might say that hey hadn't fully learned the lesson of funeral decorum, I was touched t their obvious love for their grandmother and their willingness to mbrace that sorrow.

We may wonder about Hagar's way of dealing with her despair. By valking away from Ishmael, it appears that Hagar was unwilling to do he hard work of staying with her son to comfort him and just be with im. And that may be true. But what may also be true is that Hagar was eing honest enough with herself to know that she simply couldn't bear o watch him die.

In the end, it's not up to us to judge Hagar—or ourselves—when we re in desperate waters. We might collapse or we might be a tower of ce–maiden strength. We might rant and rave or we might withdraw nto a depressed silence. It doesn't matter. Whatever our reaction, here's what's true: when I am at the end of my rope, when I simply can't do what I should be doing or what's expected of me, there is still grace and here is still God. And that, my friends, is enough.

From a Distance

Then she went and sat down opposite him a good way off, about the distance of a bowshot; for she said, "Do not let me look on the death of the child."

This is a strange passage. What were Hagar's feelings toward her son as she moved away from him and sat at a distance so she didn't have to look upon his death? We don't know the details of the journey that brought them to the meager shade of the desert bush, but our life experiences suggest some possible questions. Were they arguing, blaming each other for their predicament? I'm experienced in arguing with adolescent males, and it's not pretty. Ishmael and Hagar may have spoken harsh words to each other, or poured their anger upon the wicked stepmother (Sarah) and the abandoning father (Abraham). Did the anger and fear lead them both to tears?

Were they simply exhausted? Were they overcome with sorrow or fear? Had Ishmael, the silent one in the text, lapsed into a coma by this point, or was he delirious? Is this another example of Hagar's selfishness? Was this, as Phyllis Trible suggests, the way in which Hagar was preparing her son's deathbed? Or was it just too much for her to take?

We don't know. What we do know is that distance, for Hagar and for us, is both a blessing and a curse. For the little girl being sexually abused by her uncle, the ability to distance herself from the physical act is life–preserving, but that same response of withdrawal from her husband at age 30 is destructive to their marriage. Watching a teenage child on the path to self–destruction, we struggle between the desire to bail him out and the need to let the chips fall where they may. We wish we could shake some sense into our teens, but at the same time, we recognize that the path to adulthood is theirs to walk.

Proverbial wisdom has its clichéd perspectives on this subject that don't always agree, such as "absence makes the heart grow fonder," and "out of sight, out of mind." What we learn is that distance is something to use with care. Some smother by nature, and others do relationships in absentia. Emotional distance allows for effective care–giving and helps us see the pitfalls of dependency, but compassion must connect with another, or it is an empty act. Catholic priest Henri Nouwen offers a helpful image when he describes marriage as "a relationship that looks like two hands that fold in an act of prayer. The fingertips touch, but the hands can create a space created by love, not by fear. Marriage is creating a new, open space where God's love can be revealed."[34] Certainly that image can be applied to our parenting and friendships as well.

We also can't use distance to avoid pain. Pain is a land to be walked through, not skirted around, for pain is filled with purpose. Dr. Paul Brand and Phillip Yancey co–authored a book that describes a radical view of pain in its title: *The Gift of Pain*. They challenge us with these words: "Rather than trying to 'solve' pain, by eliminating it, we must learn to listen to it, and then manage it. That shift will require a radical change in outlook, one that cuts across the grain of American's 'we–can–fix–it' optimism."[35] A related belief is that if we ignore pain, it will go away. That may happen at times, but generally, if the underlying cause of the pain is not determined (as in a toothache or broken bone), the resulting damage will be irreversible.

Whatever factors may have played into Hagar's decision to walk away for a time, I do understand her reaction. As my own father lay in the ICU after he apparently suffered a series of strokes during surgery, a CAT scan showed no functional brain activity. We made the call to "pull the plug," but he kept breathing (a function of the autonomic portion of the brain, we were told). As a pastor, I had been in the presence of this kind of dying before, but this time it was my beloved Dad. I've got to admit, I wanted to get away. I didn't want to watch him die. I was powerless to save him, and I kept hoping that he would pass over quickly—or miraculously sit up and say, "What are you guys doing here?"

So even here, my sympathies are with Hagar. I've known parents whose children have died, and their grief has been profound, untouchable. We must wonder if Hagar instinctively knew this, and therefore needed to put some space between herself and the impending death of her child of the promise. *I cannot bear to look ...*

---

[34] Nouwen, p. 130.

[35] Paul Brand and Phillip Yancey, *The Gift of Pain*. Grand Rapids, MI: Zondervan, 1997, p. 190.

Weeping

And as she sat opposite him,
she lifted up her voice and wept.

There she goes, crying in the wilderness. In today's culture, a woman's tears have gotten a bad rap. It's messy, with runny mascara and a dripping nose. It's wimpy, for if women want to play in the sandbox in a man's world, they've learned that they can't cry at the drop of a hat. We are often ashamed of our tears and get angry with ourselves when they fall against our will. At a time when a man's tears have become more acceptable in our culture, a woman's tears are not always welcome by herself or by others.

Of course, we all know (other) women whose tears are a powerful weapon in their manipulation kit. Just cry at the right moment, and you'll get what you want. We've all witnessed it and turned away in disgust—and probably have tried it a time or two ourselves. I've recently been in a situation when I knew that tears would get me what I wanted, but using them in that way felt really cheap, so I avoided that temptation.

Tears, however, are a natural part of who we are, both as men and women. We weep from emotional stress, fear, despair, or pain—and even out of pure, overwhelming joy! Despite our culture's prejudice against weeping in public, our tears are a legitimate expression of emotion and needn't be a source of shame. There are times when our only viable eaction is to weep, to cry out to heaven, to let the tears freely flow. As Rita Schiano understands: "Tears are God's gift to us. Our holy water. They heal us as they flow."[36]

There is a striking image in Psalm 56:8, in which the psalmist suggests hat God has "put my tears in your bottle." It is unlikely that God saves ubble gum wrappers or paper clips, but he knows and saves the tears f his people. That truth gives me both comfort and hope. El–roi is resent. He is seeing.

The words that describe Hagar's weeping give us food for thought. She lifted up her voice and wept." It doesn't appear as though she was

---

Rita Schiano, *Sweet Bitter Love,* Arizona: Rising Tide Press, 1997, p. 45.

trying to hide her tears; in fact, if she lifted up her voice, either s unleashed all the pent–up emotions and wailed, or she wanted someo to hear her weep. Ah, did she want her angel—or God Almighty—to h her? What, indeed, do you do when you're desperate? There is freed in the release found in tears; a good cry, especially when someone present to hold us, can actually work wonders, both physiologically a emotionally.

Is it time that we as women learn to wail like our ancient sist did—or as our sisters of some cultures still do? A recent conversati with a friend who teaches a class for counselor training on the subj of sexual abuse was powerful. Each semester, because she recognizes t power of firsthand testimony, she asks a couple of her clients who a finished with therapy if they would tell their stories to her class. S told me that when the guest speakers left the class, there was actuall time of wailing. Some wailed for their own pain, and others for the pa that they had never truly known existed. They were taken aback by t depth of emotion while they legitimately mourned the losses they, well as the storytellers, had faced.

Forget the mascara. When our children are dying, whether in a des or on a street corner, we must wail. When our grief is overwhelmi we must wail. When there is no justice, we must wail. When we sim cannot go on, when we see no prospect of hope, when we are abandon we must wail. To save another's life, we must wail.

There is, however, a twist to this account that is troubling. God d not answer because Hagar wept (according to the narrator), but inste because he heard the cry of the boy. Now it is possible that a narrat in a highly patriarchal culture didn't want to admit that God mig have lowered himself to hear the cry of a poor, minority slave–wom Yet even in this, Hagar remains the tool in a larger story, for Ishm was the child of the promise whose life God desired to preserve. It i painful reminder that it really is not all about us. There is a larger sto being played out on a stage we cannot see, and so we close our eyes, c our tears and trust God for the outcome.

Given that the response is directed at Hagar, it may have been her so that God heard, or it may have been the whimpers of a dying boy. T important thing, the powerful truth, is that God heard and responde

God Shows Up

And the angel of God called to Hagar from heaven …

It's about time. Finally, God shows up. Weren't you waiting for him to ride to Hagar's rescue, charging in on a white horse to save the day? I date myself, but I can hear the refrain: "Here he comes to save the day! We know that Mighty Mouse is on his way!" We've been raised on superheroes and happy endings, and it is hard to think that God would have left Hagar and Ishmael to die, especially considering his promise to her.

Yet given the description of the desert, I would not have bet on Hagar in this scenario.

Here is the hard truth. We cannot predict or control God's coming—not his timing, not his method, and not his appearance. I love to hear people in their 70s and 80s talk about this walk of faith, and how, over the course of a long life, God would make his presence known to them. Sometimes there was a pattern that they could see. One woman told me the role of fasting in her life as a way of getting closer to God. Another friend deliberately sought a wilderness experience from time to time, for he knew that when he wasn't distracted by the details of day–to–day living, he was more aware of God. But for others, the presence of the Lord came when least expected.

A recently widowed friend told me of her experience:

> I was in the supermarket and reached for a box of Bran Flakes, the cereal that my husband had eaten every morning for the last thirty years. Tears sprang to my eyes as I realized, 'You don't need to buy those anymore—he's gone.' Literally, within seconds, right there in the cereal aisle of the Piggly Wiggly, the Lord was with me. I felt a sweet warmth, like a summer breeze, and I heard the echo of the promise: 'He will cover you with his feathers, and under his wings you will find refuge.'

While we cannot predict and control, we can "Prepare ye the way of the Lord," as the prophet Isaiah proclaimed. We sing of this in hymns of the faith, such as John Oxenham's picture of solitude:

> 'Mid all the traffic of the ways
> Turmoils without, within.
> Make in my heart a quiet place,
> And come and dwell within.
>
> Come, occupy my silent place,
> And make thy dwelling there,
> More grace is wrought in quietness
> Than any is aware.[37]

Our preparation might include the solitary place, but it can also be found in community. Victor Ottaway understood the role of others in the seeking of God: "Make me aware of thee, O Lord, as with thy children I unite … O Master, let thy people be consistently aware of thee."[38] In both the silent place and in community, we can be ready for his appearance.

I want to introduce a further thought here, what the Celtic Christians would call a "thin space," or *liminal* space. This is described as a place or state in which there is only the thinnest of veils between ourselves and God. Liminal space is not "church" space necessarily, although, as Franciscan priest and teacher Richard Rohr tells us, "once in a while church is liminal space, and often prepares us for it. It keeps the pot stirred so that when the fatal ingredients are dropped into the stew of life, all the necessary spices and condiments are ready to do their work."[39] Writing shortly after 9/11, he went on to say that "we must trust that this darkness, this tragic time, is also light unimaginable … This is the liminal space we have been talking about." I've got to believe that Hagar was in that thin space, with only a sheer veil between herself and God.

Sorrow, fear, or abandonment may prepare our hearts for these

---

[37] John Oxenham, *The Song Book of The Salvation Army*, #615.
[38] Victor Ottaway, *The Song Book of The Salvation Army*, #613.
[39] Richard Rohr, "Liminal space." *National Catholic Reporter*, Feb. 15, 2002.

kinds of encounters, as it did for Hagar, or they may simply appear. An encounter with the holy may come silently in a time of dryness, or it may be ours in the midst of a deep yearning for God. There are, perhaps, a few special places where heaven seems closer; if you've experienced them, you hold them closely as God places. Yet it may be in the cereal aisle of the Piggly Wiggly when God makes his presence known.

We must also recognize that sometimes God doesn't appear in any way that we can sense or feel. The shoe doesn't fit on Cinderella's foot, the cars collide, the child dies, or the house is foreclosed. There is no miracle. Then what? Then this: Sometimes he calms the storm, and sometimes he holds his child. Sometimes he comes and we absolutely know that God is present, and sometimes we only get a whiff of a scent that tells us something has changed. Whether he speaks or is silent, we can be assured by the Scriptures and the teachings of the body of Christ through the centuries that God still loves and God still cares. Turning once again to the Celts, we have the promise that is whispered in this ancient prayer of the presence of God:

> God to enfold me,
> God to surround me,
> God in my speaking,
> God in my thinking.
>
> God in my sleeping,
> God in my waking,
> God in my watching,
> God in my hoping.[40]

Traditional Celtic, Mindeman, p. 57

Fear

do not be afraid ...

As a young child, I was afraid of dogs. I don't know the genesis of that fear, but I'm guessing that a dog may have nipped at me. The fear surely did possess me. Often a well–meaning adult would say, "Don't be afraid," but those words didn't do any good, for my fear was real, and their words didn't put a muzzle on the dog. In my mind, I was still in danger, no matter how friendly the dog might appear to be.

Fear was a common reaction when God came to his people, whether he came as an angel, a messenger, or as a voice from heaven. Beginning in the creation and fall account of Genesis 1–3, we see that once Adam was exposed for what he had done, he was afraid. God recognized that emotion in other encounters as well. "Do not be afraid" were the first words of the Lord to Abraham (Gen. 15), and were echoed by Gabriel's words to Mary (Luke 1); the shepherds were described as being "sore afraid" (Luke 2, *KJV).* Let's face it, if an angel suddenly showed up at the deli counter, we'd be "sore afraid" too!

Yet, as Hagar had already been confronted by the presence of the Lord at the well that was named Beer–lahai–roi, it is more likely that the voice of God was speaking directly to Hagar's circumstances rather than to her fear of him. She certainly had reason to be afraid. She had been a slave for many years, had suffered Sarah's harsh treatment and Abraham's banishment, and now she faced a long, lonely death as well as the death of her son. Fear hits hardest when it appears as though we have no options, and that's where Hagar found herself. After the glorious promise from God, now she is down to her final breath, and she is terrified.

Fear comes in a variety of garbs: fear of failure, pain, rejection, abandonment, humiliation, and death. Listen to fear's voices:

- *If I fail one more time, I'm never going to be able to face my boss again.*
- *I am so afraid that I won't be able to deal with the pain from this illness.*

- *If I don't make the team, I don't know what I'm going to do.*
- *If I don't do what my husband says, he'll leave, and I couldn't face that.*
- *I can't bear to have them see me like this.*
- *I'm going to die, and I am so afraid.*

Whatever the color of our "fear clothes," we all have them. Some o us can take them off and discard them pretty easily. Others, though, by nature or nurture, are more fearful, as Toni Morrison describes: "Seedec in childhood, watered every day since, fear had sprouted through he veins all her life."[41]

The good news is that fear can be overcome, even if it appear overwhelming. If we are to accept the words of the Lord to Hagar fo ourselves, we can turn our backs on fear, and in its place, choose courage This theme is found numerous times in the Scriptures. Surrounc yourself with the promises of God. Memorize them. Put them on you refrigerator, on your computer screen, and on the bathroom mirror. A the writer of Proverbs suggests, "bind them round your neck, write them upon the tablet of your heart" (Prov. 3:3).

Here are a few of these promises to get you started.

- Be strong and courageous; do not be frightened or dismayed, for the Lord your God is with you wherever you go. (Josh. 1:9)
- Do not be afraid, little flock, for your Father has been pleased to give you the kingdom. (Luke 12:32, *NIV 2011)*
- The Lord is my light and my salvation; whom shall I fear? The Lord is the stronghold of my life; of whom shall I be afraid? (Ps. 27:1)
- Do not fear, for I am with you, do not be afraid, for I am your God; I will strengthen you, I will help you, I will uphold you with my victorious right hand. (Is. 41:10)
- Do not fear, for I have redeemed you; I have called you by name, you are mine. When you pass through the waters, I will

[41] Toni Morrison, *Jazz.* New York: Albert Knopf, 1992, p. 83.

be with you, and through the rivers, they shall not overwhelm you. (Is. 43:1–2)

- Don't let your hearts be troubled. Trust in God, and trust also in me. (John 14:1, *NLT)*
- For God has not given us a spirit of fear and timidity, but of power, love and self–discipline. (II Timothy 1:7, *NLT)*

This is what we need to know about fear. Fear only has as much power as we give it. It breeds in the darkness, so we can keep turning on the lights. It flourishes on ignorance, so we can get educated on whatever it is we are afraid of (cancer, divorce, doubt). We can be proactive, doing all we can to prevent the occurrence we fear—we don't need to walk down dark alleys alone at 2 a.m. We can face the consequences of the worst–case scenario, and picture ways that we could survive. When fear is overwhelming, we can get help; there are many good therapists who can work with us specifically in the area of fear.

As we begin to kick the fear monsters out from under our beds, we must be careful to fill those spaces with fear–busters. Fear cannot co–exist with love, power, self–discipline, hope, and peace. If fear is the poison, love and hope must be the antidotes. "Such love has no fear because perfect love expels all fear" (I John 4:18, *NLT).*

Naming Grief

What troubles you?

"What troubles you, Hagar?" Well, the sarcasm in me wants to answer for Hagar by saying, *O, nothing, Lord. I just love sitting in the desert, knowing that I don't have any water, and my son is going to die. Troubling me? I have nothing to be troubled about.* Fortunately for Hagar, I wasn't there to feed her that line, and the narrative does not say that Hagar answered that particular question.

Yet it is a question we tend to ask ourselves and one another. What troubles you? I am troubled by mosquitoes and sunburn, thorns on roses, and a splinter of glass in my bare foot. I am troubled by careless words and mean–spirited neighbors. I am troubled by men who abuse their wives and by addicts who destroy their bodies. I am troubled by children who are unwanted by their parents and by elderly parents who are discarded like last week's trash. I am troubled by the unequal distribution of wealth in our world and by the callous disregard for the limited resources of our planet.

I also rail against injustice and grieve when someone seemingly dies too soon. I grieve, too, over my own sin and the damage I cause to those I love by my own careless words and less–than–loving behaviors. I mourn over potential that is wasted or unseen and over lost people.

As I wrestle with this question, it brings me to the component of grief that isn't always allowed, particularly in godly Christian women's circles—anger. I spent a lot of time with a woman who had been through a horrendous experience of unfathomable betrayal, and I realized how little she talked or journaled about anger. I didn't get it—where was her outrage at what had happened to her? Was she so understanding and forgiving that it didn't exist? Or was she ignoring or denying what was true? Hagar's story at this critical point leaves me thinking, If this is what you call blessed by God, then I'll pass, thank you very much. I'm angry for her. She did what she was told, and this is what she got?

What troubles you, Hagars of today? For starters, how about unfairness, the abuse of power, abandonment, and slavery? *If indeed you are a God of mercy and justice, how could you let my child die, my husband infect me with HIV, my house burn to the ground, or my reputation be slandered in the streets or on the Internet? How could you?*

Anger is not a forbidden emotion. It must be felt, experienced, verbalized, and known. God has broad shoulders, and he can bear our anger. Read the Psalms in a contemporary paraphrase like *The Message* if you don't believe me. The danger is warned of in Ephesians 4:26 *(KJV)*: "Be ye angry and sin not." The legitimate expression of anger, rage, and wailing do not excuse us from sinning against others in our reactions or failing to ask forgiveness when we have sinned in that way.

As a therapist, I find that there is healing power in the naming of grief. I listen to pain that deeply grieves and work to help my client wrap her arms around that pain. Recently, I was talking with a woman who was telling me her story, and at one point I stopped her, took her hands, and simply said, as my tears joined hers, "I am so sorry for the many losses you have suffered." Sometimes in our desire to be strong, we minimize our losses, and we find ourselves with a deep well of unspoken grief that keeps us from living life fully.

What troubles you? I recently talked with a young woman who was in a terrible dating relationship, and when I asked her why she stayed, she told me: "He's the only person who is willing to listen to the pain and grief that I've had to face." While it would have been easy for me to say, "Get out," I realized the power of being heard and of having her grief acknowledged and felt by another.

We may not know what to say to someone who is grieving, but we cannot pretend that grief doesn't exist. We can ask, "What troubles you?" and then listen to the answer. We can remember those who are gone, and we can tell the stories of how they've touched our own lives. We can sit quietly and weep together. We can hold the pain, anger, fear, and grief of another in our praying hands.

When we come to the end of the day or sit beside Hagar's bush in the burning desert, and it seems as if no one really understands the depth of our sorrowing, we have a promise that can begin to speak its way into our despair and grief. Found in an old spiritual, its certainty gives us hope to go on.

Nobody knows the trouble I've seen
Nobody knows but Jesus
Nobody knows the trouble I've seen
Glory Hallelujah
Sometimes I'm up and sometimes I'm down
Yes Lord, you know sometimes
  I'm almost to the ground
O yes, Lord.

Nobody knows like Jesus.

A Shared Strength

... lift up the boy and hold him fast with your hand.

At a time when I was struggling with uncertainty in my life, I had a long conversation with a friend and finally demanded, "Would you please just tell me what to do, and I'll do it!" Here, the Lord gets practical: Hagar, this is what you need to do. Ishmael, probably somewhere between 13 and 17, has been with Hagar in these days of banishment. While he may have been frightened and dehydrated, a revived and refreshed Ishmael becomes the way out of the desert for Hagar. Hagar had returned to an uncertain situation in Sarah's tent in order to protect the birth of this child, yet now he can provide her with a strength that can sustain them both in the days ahead.

Wilma Ann Bailey writes:

> She is no longer alone. A seventeen–year–old Ishmael would have the skills common to men in that society, and she, of course, was skilled in the occupations of women. She and her almost–grown son can successfully face the world together and triumph, but only if she lifts him and holds him fast with her hand (power). The synergism created from the linking of the power skills, strength, and drive of the woman and the young man will ensure their survival.[42]

I love the imagery found in this verse. Lift him up, lift up what you have birthed. I have birthed much in my life, beginning with three sons. But I have also written over 200 songs, numerous poems, and eight manuscripts for books. Because of some restrictions on publication that are a part of the agreement of understanding I signed prior to ordination, my ability to find any widespread exposure for my work has been limited. Early on, I decided that my role in these circumstances

[42] Wilma Ann Bailey, "Hagar: A Model for an Anabaptist Feminist?" *The Mennonite Quarterly Review,* April 1994, p. 226.

was to faithfully write, releasing the words, images and music to the hands of others, and to the hands of God.

One manuscript was about five years old and had been rejected by what seemed to be the only viable option for publication, so back it went into the file cabinet. In the midst of living with the Hagar narrative, the whisper came: *Lift up the boy. It's time for what you birthed to be lifted up.* An e–mail asking, "Is it time?" opened the door to publication, and today, women clergy around the world are holding a book that speaks to the unique call of ministry upon their lives. It was time to lift up the baby!

What has been birthed in your heart and life that needs to be lifted up? What bushel basket needs to be thrown off so that the life–light of Christ might boldly shine through you? (Matt. 5:15–16) What talent (gift, resource, ability, item of value) needs to be dug up so that it might be lifted up and multiplied? (Matt. 25:14–30)

Oh, I can hear your response—*I'm not creative, I really don't have any talents or gifts* ... While the example of writing that I've used from my own life is a tangible one of words on paper, there is much being birthed in God's people—lift it up. Consider the following examples.

When I was a child, there were two elderly women in our church who were what was then considered old maids (ouch!). They had both been educators, and lived together into their 90s in retirement. These two sisters had decided early in life that they were going to invest in promising young people from developing countries. They financed the college education for at least a dozen young Africans—these two humble, unassuming women of faith. Lift up the boy, Miss Miller!

Lisa Thompson is a young woman who was hired by The Salvation Army to spearhead its work regarding sexual trafficking. There have been many "special interest" projects in the organization over the years, but this one has gained international attention, and it has been because of the passion and the intensity of this young woman. Women and children have been freed from sexual slavery because she was willing to "lift up the boy."

As a chaplain to the Hadleigh Employment Training Centre in the United Kingdom, Major Lynn Hills found herself in a tough spot.

Policies were being established regarding "professional distancing," that had effectively eliminated any level of physical touch with clients in the program. Hills laments:

> As chaplain, I am not part of the management structure at the centre and my heart goes out to the centre leader and management team who now have to write a workable policy on 'professional distancing.' But as they frame this policy document I want to stand up and claim the right for human response, for demonstrable human care and appropriate physical contact in our life and ministry. I want to claim the power of human touch that often speaks more than words can say—a gesture that says, 'I'm here, I care, you matter, you're valuable.'[43]

Lift up that boy, Lynn!

God is birthing encouragement, art, vision, justice, mercy, music, hope, beauty, peace, tenderness, and compassion in his sons and daughters. He is preparing eyes to see, ears to listen, and hands to touch and to work. He is calling us to a ministry, a word of grace, a monthly cup of coffee with another seeker. Lift up the boy!

This verse has a second phrase that we must hear as well: Hold him fast with your hand. There is strength in connection. Combine your strengths. A number of years ago, we established a program for women leaving the welfare rolls, and we hired two young women to work as a team. What a combination! Carie brought excitement and in–your–face challenge, while Celeste contributed a steadiness and a perceptive spirit to their work. What one didn't think of, the other did. Their combined strengths were powerful, and they were able to make accommodations for their weaknesses by knowing each other well and accepting where they needed help. They also modeled this kind of connectedness for the women they worked with, multiplying the effectiveness of their work.

Hold your birth son tight, Hagar. Persevere. The tag line from "Some Enchanted Evening" is running through my head as I write these

[43] Lynn Hills, "Heart to God, Hand to Man—Political Correctness Permitting." *The Officer,* May/June 2007, p. 36.

words: "Once you have found him, never let him go." Circumstances have worked to separate you from Ishmael, even unto death, but now you are together. It brings us to this question: Is there someone in your life that you need to be holding more tightly? As our children grow older, we find ourselves needing to let them go, so that they can develop a sense of individuality. But maybe it's time to draw them back. Your Ishmael may be a husband, a dear friend, a grandchild, or a neighbor child who just needs to be loved. *Hold him (her) fast with your hand.*

Throughout Hagar's narrative, the plaintive melodies of abandonment and distance have been prominent, but here, at last, is the opportunity to sing a new song. Here is the opportunity for Hagar's redemption: *Lift up the boy—hold him fast with your hand—you have each other.* Sing, Hagar, sing.

Open Your Eyes

God opened her eyes and she saw a well of water.

My husband is hooked on the television show "Extreme Makeover: Home Edition." For the uninitiated, it is a show in which families with special needs have a house built especially for them—in the course of one week. The family goes on vacation, comes back, and stands outside their property, which is shielded from their view by a large bus. The crowd chants, "Move that bus!" and as it pulls away, the family sees their new home for the first time. "Oh, my God" tends to be the response shouted in unison, as their eyes are opened to what has so miraculously been provided. While I find myself cringing at the easy and repetitive use of that phrase on the TV show, in Hagar's case, that response would have been particularly appropriate. *Oh … my God. You have come through for me.*

"God opened her eyes and she saw … " We have to wonder: Was the well there all along, but she couldn't see it? Or did the Lord miraculously place the well there in order to save the lives of Hagar and Ishmael? The story doesn't tell us, but either way, Hagar needed to be able to see the well in order to live.

Have you ever had God open your eyes? It's an incredible experience, similar to what psychologists call an "ah–ha" moment, in which something that has been hidden is now revealed. It can happen in a variety of ways. One is through the counsel of a friend. When we see something that our friend just doesn't get, we wonder, Should I say anything? Will she get mad if I do? If our motivation in telling her is good, if we are really "for her," then perhaps this is the way God will use to open her eyes.

A variation on this is when someone speaks a prophetic word to us. We must use care in receiving this kind of word, for while I do not doubt that God can speak in this way, there can be room for abuse in the way in which it is spoken. A practical caution is to use our own spiritual discernment as well as that of others who know us before we accept the prophetic word of a stranger as gospel truth. But God *can* use another to speak prophetically, particularly someone who knows us—someone we trust.

It may be that the Lord will allow us to dream what might be termed a prophetic dream. I don't often remember my dreams, but there was a period of about six months, during a time of unwelcome transition and upheaval, when I clearly remembered my dreams upon waking. I had been praying desperately for the Lord's guidance, and I made a point to keep a pencil and paper beside my bed, so that I could capture my dreams in the early minutes of my waking day. (Apparently, after about 10 minutes, we can't grasp our dreams any longer, unless we've made a deliberate effort to talk about them, write them down, or otherwise imprint them upon our waking minds). As I've been writing this chapter, I read back through my journal from those months, and it's absolutely amazing how prophetic those dreams have turned out to be: as to my role in the lives of other women, the kind of work that I'd be led to do, and even to the location that I find myself in today, many years later.

Other times, this eye–opening comes through a sermon or a Scripture passage that suddenly illuminates a concept that had been veiled to us. While the open–the–Bible–and–point method is not very reliable, a verse or narrative can clearly speak to something that we've been seeking. Generally, this doesn't occur in a one–shot deal. Often, there are three or four ways in which the same theme, the same message, is revealed.

In my counseling work, I've watched as the eye–opening comes slowly and when it appears in a flash. At times, it is as though layers of understanding are peeled off one at a time. In those occasions, I've been grateful to the Lord for his patience, because I've recognized that a full revelation might have been too much for my client to take. But at other times, there really is an ah–ha moment that comes from God, and that is powerful to witness. I was working with a woman in a tough marriage who was finding all kinds of ways to blame her husband for their difficulties. While he definitely had his failings, she couldn't seem to grasp that she had some responsibility for the dynamics of their relationship. In the course of one session, it was as though the scales fell from her eyes, and she began to sob bitterly, so convicted was she of her failure to love her husband. She made the switch from a victim who deserved sympathy and rescue to a woman whose eyes were opened to her own sin.

We must note that this description of Hagar's experience doesn't end with God opening her eyes, because the Lord doesn't open our eyes simply to allow us to see. There is always a greater purpose. He opens our eyes so that we can see what he has provided for us and so that we can do something with it. Our well may be that of refreshment, when we simply see the faithfulness of God and drink of that sustenance. It may be a lesson we need to learn in order to survive a dangerous situation. Our renewed vision can bring us to a needed repentance, with the well being symbolic of what Richard Rohr calls the "baptismal drowning pool," so that we can rise from its drowning waters into new life.[44] Or our enhanced vision can show us the way ahead and the direction that we can take to be obedient to God.

We often sing, "God, open our eyes." Are we ready to see what's waiting for us.

---

[44] Richard Rohr, "We Need Transformation, Not False Transcendence." *National Catholic Reporter*, Feb. 15, 2002.

Move

*She went, and filled the skin with water,
and gave the boy a drink.*

This final scene from the story of Hagar offers us a reminder that even in the midst of great distress or incredible hope, we simply must do what we have to do. Cultural messages, particularly those found in television commercials, insist that we can have it all; we can go for the gusto; and when life gets rough, we can get away. Sometimes we *can* get away, and a respite from a difficult situation can be life–saving. But most people in our world don't have four weeks paid vacation, and if they do, the paid part needs to go to pay the rent, not to buy a timeshare in the Bahamas.

Most days, when we get up, we "fill the skin with water and give the boy a drink." We prepare the meal, pay the gas bill, send the kids off to school, and head to our jobs. We do what we have to do so that our children can live, so they can have a roof over their heads and food in their bellies. There is no shame needed for being responsible, in doing what needs to be done.

Consider the example of Myrlie Evers, widow of civil rights leader Medgar Evers. Her husband was assassinated in 1963; it was one of a number of high–profile deaths in that decade. Unlike Jacqueline Kennedy, Myrlie didn't have a huge fortune, personal fame or a powerful family to buffer her walk through such a tragic loss. She didn't have the high–profile position or the family heritage of Coretta Scott King. What she had was three young children and little income. Myrlie writes of her experience:

> Life is never without struggle. For thirty years, I had painstakingly transformed myself, trading in my mantle of widowhood for a cloak of increasing independence. I relocated from Jackson, Mississippi, to Claremont, California, where I enrolled in Pomona College to earn a bachelor's degree and worked to

> survive as a single mother. By the 1970s, I had become an activist in my own right and a businesswoman, moving from the sheltered university atmosphere to corporate America and politics. I thought I could never love again, yet I found in Walter Edward Williams an equal partner and a wonderful, mature love. I watched times change; I watched my children grow to become adults; I became a grandmother. And I learned many lessons along the way.
>
> Many women today ask, 'How did you do it all?' The short answer is: A day at a time. The long answer is that I simply stayed the course with a powerful belief in God and in myself. When my strength wavered, I said to myself, *God hasn't brought you this far to leave you now*. I was able to go that last mile—for Medgar, for my children, for me—because I had courage and an abiding faith.
>
> Medgar had always made me promise to take care of 'his' children. Though I constantly reminded him that they were in fact our children, I kept my promise—and more. I took care of the family, continued his work, forged a career of my own.
> I made a difference, as Medgar had always hoped I would.[45]

Do you remember what they tell you on an airplane? In case of emergency, put the oxygen mask on yourself and then help the child that you have with you. Necessary advice in that situation, because an unconscious mother can't help her child. Yet by Hagar's example, we see that there are times when the child must be given the drink. There are times when the sacrifice must be made.

Now of course, Hagar drank from the well too. She too was thirsty and God's provision was given. The pendulum swings in a wide arc.

---

[45] Myrlie Evers–Williams, *Watch Me Fly: What I Learned on the Way to Becoming the Woman I Was Meant To Be*. New York: Little Brown and Company, 1999, p. 124.

Some mothers are pretty self–centered and make sure they have the creature comforts they need without much regard to the needs of their children. Other mothers are so self–sacrificing that their children come to believe they are absolutely entitled to everything that they want. Wise parents know that there is a balance to be found between these two extremes.

The principle extends beyond parenting, doesn't it? Whether in child–rearing, marriage, work or ministry, God provides. But the Hagar within us still needs to do her part. Whoever the parched figure in your life is, "Give the boy a drink."

A Last Glimpse

God was with the boy.

This phrase at the close of Hagar's story is a hopeful one. God did not abandon her son. The promise held true; indeed, the Lord had given heed to her affliction. As she trudged through the desert when returning to Sarah's tent, I can imagine the words tumbling through Hagar's mind: *you shall bear a son; the Lord has heard; I will multiply your offspring.* In Sarah's tent, she remembered, *the Lord has heard.* Even weeping in the desert, with her son near death, Hagar knew what God had promised. "*I will* ... "

Have you ever clung to the words of another? I have a letter from a beloved mentor that is barely intact, for I opened it and reread it numerous times. It began, "it is all right," which gave me permission to find my own way in a world that seemed less than hospitable to me. It's been quite a while since I've read it, perhaps because my midlife mind has internalized the words to the extent that I don't need the page they're written on any longer. But for many years, they carried me through days of indecision and uncertainty. Did my friend have any idea how powerful those words would be? Probably not. They were thoughtfully written, but in themselves, they were just words on paper. But for a young woman who was searching for some touchstone, they were life–giving.

It is a good reminder that the words we speak and write can carry great power, both for good and for evil. We must use care in what we say, but also can be intentional in speaking words of blessing to others. God's message comes not only through Scripture, but also through the words of his people in our day.

We also can claim words of promise for ourselves and for the Ishmaels of our lives. Just as God promised Hagar, so too he promises to be with us, to guide us, and to keep us. We've looked at a number of passages of Scripture that provide us with a variety of promises, and they can be committed to memory and held dear.

Also valuable is the claiming of songs that can uphold us. One favorite of mine is based on Psalm 91 as understood by Michael Joncas:

And He will raise you up on eagle's wings,
Bear you on the breath of dawn,
Make you to shine like the sun,
And hold you in the palm of His Hand.[46]

A final consolation and confirmation is image. God often paints pictures that can sustain us, even when we can't find a word to speak. There are many throughout the Bible, but it is Hagar's spring, the gift of a well, and the promise of water for the thirsty that is the abiding image from her narrative. One more reminder that says, *I will be with you.*

The last glimpse we get of Hagar is in Gen. 21:21. "While he (Ishmael) was living in the Desert of Paran, his mother got a wife for him from Egypt." Ishmael's life parallels that of Isaac, yet with its own twist. Both were children of promise, and both were destined to be the father of many descendants. But the way that promise played out was to be quite different, for Isaac was the child of the covenant with the Lord. As such, Abraham sent his servant to get a wife for Isaac from among his own relatives (Gen. 24). Had Sarah still been alive, I'm sure she would have had a hand in this selection, but she was dead before this took place. Thus began the story of the patriarchs of the Israelites: Abraham, Isaac, Jacob, and Joseph.

The task of finding a wife for Ishmael fell to Hagar, and here, she returned to what she knew, and brought a woman to Ishmael from her ancestors, from Egypt. She protected his life by returning to Sarah's tent; she lifted up the boy and gave him water to drink to save his life in the desert; and now she connects him to his Egyptian heritage. It's possible that the failure to find a Hebrew wife for Ishmael is indicative of the lack of involvement on the part of Abraham in Ishmael's adult life, but that's speculation at best. Ishmael did become the father to many (Gen. 25:12–18) and apparently was reconciled enough to his father and brother that he was at the burial of Abraham: "His sons Isaac and Ishmael buried him in the cave of Machpelah … " (Gen. 25:9).

While the end of our story confirms that God was with the boy, I have to believe that God was with Hagar as well. We don't know what her life was like after her encounters with the Lord, but is it possible

[46] Michael Joncas, "On Eagle's Wings." New Dawn Music, 1979.

to come face to face with God and not be changed? Even if she was physically separated from Abraham's nomadic company, she would forever carry the memory of the God who knew her name, who called her by a spring, who gave her a promise, who found her in the desert, and who opened her eyes to a well of life.

If Only

I find myself coming to the end of Hagar's story and wishing that it had ended differently. I'll admit it—I am a dreamer, and I like happy endings. I wonder what it might have been like if, at any one of the critical junctures in this account, those involved had reached for the best within themselves and responded to each other with compassion? What if Hagar had not gloated over her pregnancy? What if Sarah had not "dealt harshly" with her servant? What if Abraham had put his foot down and demanded that Sarah and Hagar get along? What if Sarah had named her feelings of envy and jealousy for what they were and chosen to extend grace? What if Abraham had refused to banish his wife and son to the desert to please Sarah? What might have changed?

Think of Isaac and Ishmael, Judaism and Islam, Israelis and Arabs. Could the course of history been changed by a kindness shown, a mercy offered? Phyllis Trible dreams with me: "The two women, caught in a patriarchal bind, might draw closer together. But that is not to be."[47]

Playing the "what if" game is a dangerous exercise. Regrets can easily lead to bitterness, and we do not have the ability to change what has already happened. Yet is there a lesson to be learned in what didn't happen? Surely there is for Sarah and Hagar, just as there is in our own lives, for every time we fail to extend a hand of care, a hand of mercy, we change the course of our lives and those of the other.

It is easy to say, *This is God's story, and he directed every action in it*, and yet, somehow, I don't see God working that way. Did the Lord cringe at some of the behaviors of his chosen people? Of course he did. The Old Testament is filled with God's longing for his people and their stiff–necked response.

But this does lead to another question: Has God designed the world in such a way that even sinful choices can be redeemed? If God redeems

Phyllis Trible and Letty M. Russell, *Hagar, Sarah and Their Children*. Louisville, KY: Westminster Knox Press, 2006.

the desert places, for Hagar and for Sarah, for Isaac and for Ishmael, then we can have hope. Because if God can work in their lives, he can redeem my desert places, both the deserts I am forced into and the deserts I willingly choose.

I suppose it depends upon how we see God's path for us. How do we understand a verse such as Jeremiah 29:11 *(TNIV)*: "I know the plans I have for you, declares the Lord, plans to prosper you and not to harm you, plans to give you hope and a future." Written to a people in exile, it is clear that God's initial plan would have been for the people of Israel to be faithful to him, which most likely would have kept them from exile.

Is the plan of God so fixed that if we take one step off the road, it is therefore ruined forever? I am a football fan and have watched as the ball–carrier inadvertently steps out of bounds or is pushed out of bounds, and the play is over. I'm afraid that we are quick to have that mentality—that if we fall, we're done. Yet the football player who is not carrying the ball can go out of bounds and return to make a tackle. And they can all return on the next play, for their boundary violation has been wiped clean with a new snap of the ball.

Indeed, there is a Redeemer. The master plan, the meta–narrative, did not conclude with Isaac or Ishmael. Its story threaded its way to Egypt and back, through other deserts, and into Bethlehem. It returned briefly to Egypt, only to conclude—or begin—on a desolate hillside outside the city of Jerusalem.

In the story of redemption, we know that God is in control. In the love of Jesus, we find that God sees and knows. In the compassionate modeling of Christ, we understand that God cares for his people. In the coming of the Comforter, we recognize that God keeps his promises. As it was for Hagar, so it will be for us. The well awaits, and Alber Orsborn's words provide the ladle:

> Light, life and love are in that healing fountain,
> All I require to cleanse me and rcstorc;
> Flow through my soul, redeem its desert places,
> And make a garden there for the Lord I adore.[48]

[48] Albert Orsborn, *The Song Book of The Salvation Army*, #647.

Other books by *JoAnn Streeter Shade*

Heartwork of Hope: ***A Directed Journal*** FROM OTHERS PRESS

Shade takes the reader on an interactive journey of discovery—through Scripture, poetry, and her own experiences. Dr. Jerry Flora of Ashland Theological Seminary calls Heartwork "a treasure to mine and a trail to follow."

Seasons: ***A Woman's Calling to Ministry*** FROM SALVATION BOOKS

In this book, Shade, who is a major in The Salvation Army, explores the distinct challenges women officers face through the changing seasons of their lives. Says Commissioner Helen Clifton, "Major JoAnn Shade writes reflectively in her engaging book, not about the Army's history and achievements … but a more thoughtful, individual and totally up–to–date account of what it feels like to be called of God, with high and holy thoughts, but grounded in the reality of everyday living."

Also from *Others Press*

As Far as You Can Go and Still Be in God's Hands:
Letters from Papua New Guinea

Marcia Cocker and her husband, Jim, majors in The Salvation Army, spent three years as missionary officers in Papua New Guinea. Says Colonel James Condon of the Army's Australia Eastern Territory, "Marcia Cocker has a special aptitude for writing the most interesting enjoyable, and expressive letters.... I know that readers will be captured by these writings … "

We Are …

This colorful hard–cover book, which includes 4 CDs to accompany each section, is a perfect gift for family, donors, volunteers—anyone you want to help to understand The Salvation Army. Through stunning photographs and lyrical text, including quotes from Army notables, *We Are …* presents the Army as a people of *Praise*, *Prayer*, *Power*, and *Promise*.

My New Song

Carole Jeanne Bate, a Salvation Army major, has written this book of poetry fresh from her experience. Says worship songwriter and recording artist Phil Laeger, "She is truly a warrior poet, prayerfully blazing a trail through the hardships of Christian living, giving utterance to the soul's longing for redemptive expression. You'll also not want to miss the accompanying CD, which pairs music nicely with some of Carole's poetry."

Monday Morning Motivators: *Spirit Boosters for Stressed Believers*

David Cedervall, a retired Salvation Army major, has written this book of short devotions as encouragement for pastors and church leaders, for whom Sunday is often the most intense, stress–filled day of the week. David's prayer is that these "Spirit Boosters" will be a help to any Christian, whether ordained or not, who is living out a calling from God.

Will You Choose Joy? *Reflections on Philippians*

This book, edited by Lois Rader from Normajean Honsberger's sermon series on Philippians, is laced with "Closer to Home" insights that will help readers face life's trials. Normajean, a Salvation Army officer, died after an eight–year battle with cancer, during which time she also lost her husband, but she always embraced joy. Says Pastor Jim Cymbala of Brooklyn Tabernacle, "*Will You Choose Joy?* Is a timely reminder that to be without God's joy is to miss His purpose for our lives."

Soldiers of Uncommon Valor:
A History of Salvationists of African Descent

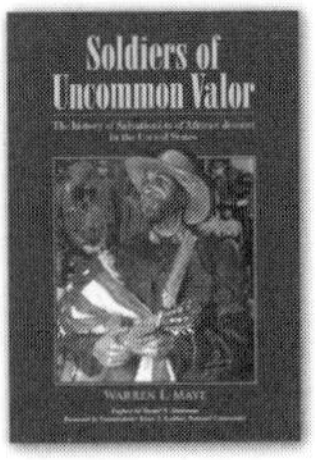

Warren L. Maye mines a rich lode of Salvation Army history. He takes the reader back to the Army's beginnings in the U.S. and explores the struggles and triumphs of African–American Salvationists from the 1800s to the present day.

Symbala's River

Stephen Kelly weaves story and Scripture together in this young people's Christian adventure novel about Symbala, age 12, who sets out to discover the source of the River that gives life to her Village. On the way Symbala begins to recall the words of the Wisewoman who raised her. Those words from Scripture lead Symbala to the end of her quest—and her destiny.

To order, call The Salvation Army at 888–488–4882. Most books are also available through www.shopsalvationarmy.org.